HOLY FIRE

Colin Urquhart

HODDER AND STOUGHTON
LONDON   SYDNEY   AUCKLAND   TORONTO

British Library Cataloguing in Publication Data

Urquhart, Colin
  Holy fire.
  1. Holy Spirit
  I. Title
  231'.3   BT121.2
  ISBN 0 340 34280 3

To Edward England, who in his loving and gracious way, has been a constant source of encouragement to me in this ministry of writing.

Acknowledgments

My deep and sincere thanks to the elders of the Bethany Fellowship, Michael Barling, David Brown, Bob Gordon and Charles Sibthorpe, as well as the members of my own household, for all the encouragement they have given me in the writing of this book. Particular thanks to Annette who has patiently typed and retyped and, of course, to my family – Caroline, my wife, Claire, Clive and Andrea; all of whom have shown such love and patience while Dad has been wrapped up in his writing!

Needless to say, it is the Lord Himself who has sustained me in what has proved to be a very demanding task. My prayer is that this book, inadequate as it inevitably is in dealing with 'Holy Fire', will be used by Him for His glory and will encourage those who read it to draw nearer to Him in His holy love.

Contents

1. FIRE

An increasing number of people are praying for revival, for a spiritual awakening to sweep through their nation. There is widespread faith that God is preparing for such a time when the holy fire of His love will fill the lives of many who do not know Him. Revival, however, has to begin among God's own people, those who already acknowledge faith in Jesus Christ. It is their hearts that need to be revived so they become effectively leaven in the lump, salt for the earth and light for the world. They cannot pray meaningfully for the Lord to meet with others unless they are prepared for Him to meet with them first.

How can we meet with the Lord so that His holy fire can cleanse our hearts and revive us with His love? We need to understand, first, that "fire" is used in a variety of ways in the Bible.

"FIRE" DESCRIBES GOD HIMSELF

A pillar of fire signifies His presence with His people in the wilderness. He met with Moses on Mount Sinai which was "covered with smoke, because the Lord descended on it in fire". (Ex. 19:18) To the Israelites His glory looked like a consuming fire on top of the mountain. (Ex. 24:17) When He revealed His glory to them, "Fire came out from the presence of the Lord and consumed the burnt offering and the fat portions on the altar. And when all the people saw it, they shouted for joy and fell face down." (Lev. 9:24)

God chose Israel to be His own people and made a covenant, a binding agreement, with them to bless them if they remained faithful and obedient to Him. He warned them not to forget this covenant or wander from His ways, "For the Lord your God is a consuming fire, a jealous God." (Deut. 4:24)

Isaiah describes the Lord's tongue as a "consuming fire" and warns: "See, the Lord is coming with fire . . . For with fire and with his sword the Lord will execute judgment upon all men." (Is. 66:15,16)

Fire, then, is used both to purge away sin and as the means of executing judgment. "He will be like a refiner's fire," Malachi says. (3:2)

Jesus Himself also warns of the fire of God's judgment: "The Son of Man will send out his angels, and they will weed out of his kingdom everything that causes sin and all who do evil. They will throw them into the fiery furnace, where there will be weeping and gnashing of teeth." (Matt. 13.41–2)

Whatever Jesus means by that it does not sound too encouraging! By contrast, "the righteous will shine like the sun in the kingdom of their Father" (v. 43).

"FIRE" IS USED TO DESCRIBE HELL

Clearly God wants His children to be righteous and to enjoy their heavenly inheritance. So Jesus warns of the dire consequences of sin that can destroy that inheritance: "If your hand or your foot causes you to sin, cut it off and throw it away. It is better for you to enter life maimed or crippled than to have two hands or two feet and be thrown into eternal fire. And if your eye causes you to sin, gouge it out and throw it away. It is better for you to enter life with one eye than to have two eyes and be thrown into the fire of hell." (Matt. 18:8–9)

Drastic measures indeed! Obviously the "fire of hell" is so awful people must be warned to avoid it at all costs. However, Jesus wants them not only to avoid hell but to experience His life fully and to know what it is to live in Him. Then their lives will be fruitful in the way His Father intends. However, "If anyone does not remain in me, he is

like a branch that is thrown away and withers; such branches are picked up, thrown into the fire and burned." (John
15:6)

Again He draws the contrast for the faithful and obedient: "If you remain in me and my words remain in you,
ask whatever you wish, and it will be given you. This is to
my Father's glory, that you bear much fruit, showing
yourselves to be my disciples." (John 15:7–8)

So there will come the separating of the sheep from the
goats when Jesus comes in His glory. The sheep, those who
have followed Him faithfully, will receive their inheritance
of God's Kingdom; but to the goats He will say: "Depart
from me, you who are cursed, into the eternal fire prepared
for the devil and his angels." (Matt. 25:41) The disobedient
will go to eternal punishment, "but the righteous to eternal
life." (v. 46) Jesus says the fire never goes out in hell.

"FIRE" DESCRIBES THE ACTIVITY OF GOD'S HOLY SPIRIT

Fire also speaks of the Holy Spirit's activity within the
Christian. "Do not put out the Spirit's fire," Paul urges. (1
Thess. 5:19) For the Spirit will inspire love and zeal for
God's ways and will effect the purging out of sin and evil
from the heart. By working within him, the Lord will fit the
Christian for heaven.

John the Baptist prophesied of Jesus: 'He will baptize
you with the Holy Spirit and with fire." (Luke 3:16) Being
immersed in the Spirit of God will lead to the believer's
heart being inflamed with love for God; but will also subject
him to His cleansing, purging, refining power.

"FIRE" WILL TEST EACH MAN'S WORK

The Day of the Lord will bring to light the nature of each
man's work, Paul says. "It will be revealed with fire, and
the fire will test the quality of each man's work. If what he
has built survives, he will receive his reward. If it is burned
up, he will suffer loss; he himself will be saved, but only as
one escaping through the flames." (1 Cor. 3:13–15)

Fire purges, consumes and tests. Becoming a Christian is not the completion of God's purpose for the believer. He wants him to build and be fruitful so that his work survives the testing.

Jesus Himself will be "revealed from heaven in blazing fire with his powerful angels." (2 Thess. 1:7) Those who love the Lord will not need to fear His coming for they know they shall be taken to rejoice with Him in His glory. However, "if we deliberately keep on sinning after we have received the knowledge of the truth, no sacrifice for sins is left, but only a fearful expectation of judgment and of raging fire that will consume the enemies of God." (Heb. 10:26–7)

The Christian does not need to live in fear of judgment, only in awe of God, his holy and almighty Father who has shown such love, mercy and grace to him. "Therefore, since we are receiving a kingdom that cannot be shaken, let us be thankful, and so worship God acceptably with reverence and awe, for our God is a consuming fire." (Heb. 12:28–9)

The believer will not resent the refining; he is only too conscious of the need for it. It may come through various difficulties or trials. These God allows, "So that your faith – of greater worth than gold, which perishes even though refined by fire – may be proved genuine and may result in praise, glory and honour when Jesus Christ is revealed." (1 Pet. 1:7)

Peter advises: "You ought to live holy and godly lives as you look forward to the day of God and speed its coming. That day will bring about the destruction of the heavens by fire, and the elements will melt in the heat. But in keeping with his promise we are looking forward to a new heaven and a new earth, the home of righteousness." (2 Pet. 3:11–13) We cannot imagine the immense power of this fire that will destroy the elements. No wonder Jude urges his readers: "Snatch others from the fire and save them." (v. 23)

In the Book of Revelation, the Lord is described as having eyes like blazing fire. (1:14, 2:18) The Spirit counsels the church in Laodicea to "buy from me gold refined in the fire, so you can become rich." (3:18) Better that refining than the lake of fire which is the second death. (20:14) "If anyone's name was not found written in the book of life, he was thrown into the lake of fire." (20:15)

Jesus came to give men that life and to save them from the eternal judgment they deserved because of their sin. How could the holy, righteous, just, perfect God be made one with sinners? How could they be saved from the lake of fire and be made like the Lord instead? How can the holy fire of God's love purge and cleanse their lives making them fit for heaven?

It is obvious that we have the option of inviting the refining fire of God's love in our lives now, or of experiencing the fire of His judgment later. Better the refining! Although this is a process needed in our lives, we do not necessarily welcome it. In the following pages we will be concentrating on the refining that God desires to bring into our lives through the holy fire of His Spirit. Do not resist what He wants to do in you; He has your welfare, as well as His glory, at heart.

I counsel you to buy from me gold refined in the fire, so you can become rich.

2. GREAT EXPECTATIONS

We know what we want: to be respected, admired, and loved, with sufficient money for our needs and enough to indulge ourselves in particular interests. Spiritually, we want to know the reality of God's love for us, His acceptance of us and His presence with us.

We might feel deeply about the way public worship should be ordered or the local church administered. We might want to impress upon others the truth of our own doctrinal positions and emphases. What we have perceived, all men need to perceive, what we have known all others should know, what we have received as revelation is surely intended for everyone!

We can agree that our knowledge is only partial and our understanding limited; but we experience frustration if others do not grasp at least as much of the truth as we have received, and are immediately suspicious of anyone claiming personal revelation that has eluded us.

Yet many know deep within themselves a spiritual hunger that is not satisfied by what is happening around them. How can one define this hunger? For some it may be a basic longing for the reality of a personal relationship with God; for others a desire to understand the purpose of their lives, or to see their prayers being answered. It may be that their inner dissatisfaction can only be summed up by saying, "I know there is something more."

Such a longing may be mingled with dread, a desire to draw nearer to God and yet a fear of the consequences of doing so. There may be an awareness that not all is as it should be spiritually, but bewilderment as to how things could be improved. This can lead to self-condemning feelings of failure or to futile attempts to justify oneself. Are others any better off? Nobody is perfect, after all!

And yet there is a fear that others are more genuine in their faith and less hypocritical in their attitudes. Do other Christians experience the same base desires and unholy longings? Do their minds run wild with sexual fantasies or do they dream of being highly esteemed and revered by others? Do they know the same emptiness in prayer? Do they know what it is to speak of spiritual things while longing to experience the very things of which they speak?

THE VITAL QUESTION

What does God expect of me? Perhaps that is the most dreaded question of all. It is much easier to face what the Church expects of me, what my pastor expects of me, what my fellow Christians expect of me. It is easier to tell God what I expect of Him, wanting Him to dance to my tune. Let Him watch over me and love me and comfort me and forgive me and provide for me. I will worship Him; I will pray to Him; I will serve Him. But please, please, don't let Him ask too much of me.

We justify such attitudes by saying: "God has given me my life; it is mine. I will acknowledge the Lord, respect Him, love Him as far as I am able and regard the way I run my life as serving Him. He doesn't expect to be intimately involved in the details of my life. He has more important things to do. There are others who need Him more than I, those who are in desperate situations."

How far we are from understanding the truth about God and His purposes for us if we believe such reasoning.

The very question that each of us needs to face is: "What do you expect of me, Lord?" What does He want to do with your life? Are you fulfilling His expectations? You need not fear to ask such questions of God. He does not expect anything of you without making available His own rich resources of supply to enable you to fulfil His plans. To desire His purposes is to desire Him. The man who tries to serve God without knowing Him is defeating His own ends.

It is easy to fill our lives with activities and religious exercises, all of which have little or nothing to do with His desires for us and His expectations of us.

He wants us to have great expectations of Him because He is the Almighty God. He also has great expectations of His children, far greater than most realise. What is more, He promises that those expectations will be fulfilled; He will ensure that. He holds out to us the very resources that we need to please Him. What a waste it would be to reach the end of our earthly lives without ever discovering why God had made us. How frustrating for the Creator and futile for the created ones!

How much better to know Him and His purposes, to hear Him say: "Well done, good and faithful servant! You have been faithful with a few things; I will put you in charge of many things. Come and share your master's happiness!" (Matt. 25:21)

God desires the best for you, to enable you to enter the rich inheritance He has prepared for you. He wants your joy to be full. He wants to refine out of your life all the things that hinder His best purpose for you. But He needs your cooperation to do that.

HIS PURPOSE

When parents look into the face of their new-born child they experience several emotions. They feel love, joy and relief at the infant's safe delivery. At the same time they are aware how weak and frail the baby seems, how defenceless and utterly reliant on those who will care for him. They become deeply conscious of their responsibilities towards the baby; his life is in their hands.

They also have desires for the child. They want to provide the best possible upbringing for him. They will pass on to him their own priorities, beliefs, attitudes and ways of life. They may have a career in mind for him, to follow in father's footsteps, perhaps. Or they may want something better for him than they have ever known themselves.

They will have to feed, clothe and care for the child; but also they will be largely responsible for shaping his development as a person. At times that will prove challenging and demanding, as the boy begins to develop in personality and wants to exercise his independent self-will. He will need correction and discipline as well as affection.

The parents hope their son will turn out to be a credit to them, a young man who returns the love they have given him, who has learned to be responsible and self-disciplined, whose integrity is respected by all who know him.

Does the heavenly Father look for anything less in His children? He regards them with love and joy. He is devoted to their well-being and knows how dependent they are on Him; their lives are in His hands. He wants the best possible upbringing for them; He desires to pass on to them His own priorities, beliefs, attitudes and way of life. He has careers in mind for them, following in His Fatherly footsteps. He wants to shape the development of their personalities, correcting and disciplining them in love when they are tempted to act independently of Him.

He desires His children to be a credit to Him, men and women who respond to His love with loving obedience and who are responsible, self-disciplined people of integrity.

God has made you in His own image and intends you to be like Him. Whatever He is, He desires you to be so that you will reflect His character in the world, a child of God manifesting the love and faithfulness of his or her heavenly Father. "But just as he who called you is holy, so be holy in all you do; for it is written: 'Be holy, because I am holy.'" (1 Pet. 1:15–16)

TO BE HOLY IS TO BE LIKE JESUS

In His earthly ministry Jesus revealed His Father in all He said and did. "Anyone who has seen me has seen the Father," he said. (John 14:9) "It is the Father, living in me, who is doing his work." (v. 10) In Jesus we see the outworking of a holy life, what it means to live God's life in the world with all its opposition to holiness. He demonstrates that holiness is not a restricted life of legalistic bondage, but life lived to the full, overflowing with love, joy, and power.

All Christians are called to live God's life in the world. Although they will not do this as perfectly as Jesus, nevertheless He makes it possible for them to reflect something of His personality and to live in ways which please Him. He came to give them the fullness of His life.

HOLINESS

Because Jesus is holy, His followers are to be holy; they are to be like Him. To live a holy life, the Christian needs to be full of Jesus, full to overflowing with His love, life, joy and power. To attempt to live a godly life through his own efforts will certainly end in frustration and failure.

The individual believer who fears holiness may want to receive the blessings that come with new life in Jesus, but he does not want to face the implications of true discipleship. "Be holy" comes as a direct command from the Lord and cannot be easily laid aside as an unattainable desire on His part, or as an option for particularly pious people. If God is holy, then His children are to be holy.

Holiness is often ridiculed as "old-fashioned", "out-of-date" morality. Within large sections of the Church it is shunned, largely because many have tried to produce a Gospel acceptable to the world. They have reduced God to some beneficent heavenly uncle who smiles lovingly upon His world, ever patient about people's sins and wanting to assure them they will be all right in the end!

As the perfect Father, God is too concerned about the welfare of His children to leave them undisciplined. Sin is extremely serious to Him; it prevents His children being like Him and destroys their lives. And if a man believes he is heaven-bound when he is not, he is deceived.

It is tempting to regard holiness as something totally beyond us, to believe that such a state can only belong to heaven and could not be attained this side of the grave, at least not by ordinary people. This shows a misunderstanding of holiness. In Jesus, God has already made the believer holy in His sight and has given him all that is necessary to enable him to live in holiness.

The Christian will miss the heart of God's purpose for him if he does not want to be holy. There is no deeper desire in God's heart for His children than this; only then will they reflect His own character and do what pleases Him.

If you truly want the holiness of the Lord in your life, you will be prepared to face your unholiness, painful though that may be, for it is sin that prevents God's life being seen more fully in you. Holiness will not be created by looking in upon yourself; it is not achieved by withdrawing from the world, taking vows of poverty or subjecting yourself to arduous ascetical practices. It is the result of drawing nearer to God so that more of His life can be seen in you, that you may be able to live the life of Jesus more fully.

God is infinitely higher and greater than anything we could imagine him to be. "To whom will you compare me? Or who is my equal? says the Holy One." (Is. 40:25) We are so tainted by sin, we cannot understand the holiness of God, that He is perfect and complete in Himself.

And yet we are told to "seek the Lord while he may be found; call on him while he is near." (Is. 55:6) Although He is so much greater than we are, He desires to reveal Himself to us. As we draw nearer to Him, we will become increasingly aware of our unholiness by comparison, for no one is like this God who is majestic in holiness. At the same time we will know the assurance of His love and forgiveness and His victory in those areas of our lives that do not reflect His holiness, for He will continue to refine us with His holy fire.

Seek the lord while he may be found, call on him while he is near.

3. MADE IN HIS IMAGE

"Then God said, 'Let us make man in our image, in our likeness . . .' So God created man in his own image, in the image of God he created him; male and female he created them." (Gen. 1:26,27) However literally you interpret the opening chapters of Genesis, what God teaches through the creative narrative is clear. He told Adam and Eve not to eat of the tree of knowledge of good and evil. While they remained obedient they could enjoy fellowship with Him and were able to reflect His holiness. Disobedience reduced them to a state of sinfulness. Immediately their natural reaction was to hide from God; they had lost their innocence before Him and one another.

They discovered nothing could be hidden from His eyes and that sin is so grievous to Him they were immediately banished from the Garden of Eden, the place where they had enjoyed the beauty of fellowship with their Creator. Just one act of disobedience had such dire consequences.

Sin still has the same results. It divides and separates man from the One who made him and prevents him from being able to fulfil the purpose of his existence. How can a sinner reflect the image of God in whom there is no sin? The image is immediately marred and the purpose of God frustrated.

This is the common condition of all people, for, "All have sinned and fall short of the glory of God." (Rom. 3:23) Sin is the disease that affects every person and every part of their souls – their minds, wills and emotions. It is tempting to believe that sin is not as bad as God says it is, that disobedience to what God has said does not matter.

It mattered so much to God that He sent His Son to the world to suffer crucifixion to undo the consequences of sin. Jesus had to live a life of total obedience to His Father, to atone for the disobedience of Adam, Eve and every other human being.

EXPOSING WHAT IS WITHIN

Cain was jealous of his brother, Abel. The Lord had accepted Abel's offering but rejected Cain's. That rejection did not create the anger, jealousy and hatred that led to Cain violently killing his brother. The rejection of his offering simply exposed the driving force of sin in Cain's heart. "Why are you angry? Why is your face downcast? If you do what is right, will you not be accepted? But if you do not do what is right, sin is crouching at the door; it desires to have you, but you must master it." (Gen. 4:6–7)

We want to blame the difficult circumstances for the negative ways in which we react. God allows difficulties so that sinful motives and desires locked away within us become exposed. Sinful reactions are the consequences of what we are, not what happens to us. That is why different people will react in different ways when in identical situations.

The lives of men, women and children are built around "self": self-pleasing, self-concern, self-preservation, selfishness, self-pity. All are negative and destructive in their effects upon the individual and those around him.

The first act of sin was a conscious decision to please self and so displease God by directly disobeying His command. That is still the nature of sin; it has just as far-reaching consequences. To God any sin in our lives is as awful as that first act of disobedience. It merits our being cast out of paradise and separated from fellowship with God.

He does not have any double standards; to the Lord sin is always awful. He does not think in terms of little sins and big sins, of white sins and black sins. Sin is sin; it is opposition to His will and disobedience to His commands. Its consequences must be faced.

SIN IN A CHRISTIAN

A Christian knows that Jesus is his Saviour and has forgiven all his past sins. He is constantly thankful that he can be cleansed by the precious blood of Jesus shed for him. However, many wrongly suppose that God's view of their present and future sin will be different; that He will have a more lenient attitude now they are His children. Having experienced His forgiveness they presume upon Him.

God views sin in a Christian's life with greater gravity, and yet with infinite patience. An unbeliever may not know what God requires of him, but the Christian should know better and has been given resources to resist temptation. He cannot reflect the image of God while he sins, neither can he walk in fellowship with his Lord. Jesus cannot be seen in his pride, selfishness, anger, bitterness or jealousy. He is not present in his lust and greed. "Those who live like this will not inherit the kingdom of God," Paul warns. (Gal. 5:21)

Like Cain, it is natural to resent the setbacks we experience because they reveal what is wrong with our hearts. You can imagine you are free of jealousy until you see in someone else a quality you desire. You are not angry unless someone upsets you. You may think yourself incapable of hate until you are hurt deeply by somebody. "The good man brings good things out of the good stored in his heart, and the evil man brings evil things out of the evil stored up in his heart. For out of the overflow of his heart his mouth speaks". (Luke 6:45)

The Lord wants to refine you so that when tempted you will respond, not like Adam and Eve, but like Jesus. All Christians need to heed the warning to Cain: "But if you do not do what is right, sin is crouching at your door; it desires to have you, but you must master it!"

When you make conscious decisions to please yourself and disobey God's word, you grieve Him deeply. If you truly want His purpose for your life, you desire to be finished with sin and want to be holy.

HOLINESS IS POSITIVE

Holiness is more than the absence of what displeases God. It is positive. To be holy is to be like God, to reflect Him in heart, thoughts, attitudes, speech and actions. That is only possible when we not only turn away from sin, but desire to put on Christ, to be filled with His life, love and power. For God does not command us to be holy in our own strength by our own human efforts, but by allowing the Spirit of His holiness to radiate from our hearts in our personalities and actions.

Holiness is to be full of Jesus.

A church-going woman was heard to remark: "I'm not sure that I want to be holy." She gave the impression that the very idea was outrageous. Was she a Christian, or had she never truly understood God's purpose for her life?

Holiness is God's purpose for you; He has no lesser purpose for you or for any Christian. "Without holiness no one will see the Lord." (Heb. 12:14) It is His purpose that one day you will see Him face to face, and be like Him. Then His plan for you will be completed.

BE HOLY BECAUSE I AM HOLY

We will become holy, not by concentrating on the negative but on the positive. There is nothing negative about God or His Son, Jesus, who expresses His life perfectly. He has given us His Holy Spirit so that His holy life might be expressed in us.

The Kingdom of God reflects the nature of the King who reigns over it. Because the Lord is positive, everything about His Kingdom is positive. Jesus is the Way to that Kingdom, which is founded on truth. He came to give us the life of that Kingdom, which Paul says is "righteousness, peace and joy in the Holy Spirit" (Rom. 14:17). It is the Kingdom of love and power and light.

He wants our lives to be founded on these principles so

that we can oppose victoriously all the negative temptations and pressures to which we are subjected. For there is another spiritual kingdom where the prince of this world rules. His kingdom is not founded on positive principles because he is himself negative. He is the thief who wants to steal, destroy and kill. He has been a liar from the beginning, is the father of all lies, the deceiver, the accuser of the brethren. Everything about him and his kingdom is negative for he has rebelled against the Lord and is determined to undermine faith by tempting God's children to be negative, thus denying the truth and inheritance they have in Jesus.

As a Christian you are to reflect the nature of King Jesus and live according to the positive principles of the Kingdom of God. "Do not be afraid, little flock, for your Father has been pleased to give you the kingdom." (Luke 12.32)

So the Lord will want to empty you of the negative and fill you with the positive. The Holy Spirit convicts you of what is negative and opposed to Jesus so that you may repent of those things, be forgiven and have your sins (which are all negative) removed from you. He wants you to know that the power of sin is broken in your life because of what He has done for you on the Cross.

Having been emptied of the negative He constantly fills you with the positive. The Holy Spirit produces in our lives the positive qualities of God and His Kingdom. "The fruit of the spirit is love, joy, peace, patience, kindness, goodness, faithfulness, gentleness and self-control." (Gal. 5:22–23) These contrast dramatically with the negative acts of the sinful nature, "sexual immorality, impurity and debauchery; idolatry and witchcraft; hatred, discord, jealousy, fits of rage, selfish ambition, dissensions, factions and envy; drunkenness, orgies, and the like." (Gal. 5:19–20)

Paul continues: "I warn you, as I did before, that those who live like this will not inherit the kingdom of God," because all those negative things are opposed to the positive qualities of the Kingdom. Therefore, they do not need to be part of the lives of those who are Christians, to whom God has chosen to give the Kingdom.

God wants our lives to be full of the Holy Spirit. "Live by the Spirit, and you will not gratify the desires of the sinful nature." (Gal. 5:16) The Holy Spirit enables us to live positively as the children of the Kingdom and Jesus makes it clear that He came so men's lives could be filled with God's life.

Jesus confronted the Pharisees with the fact that, no matter what they appeared to be externally, inwardly they were full of darkness, greed, self-indulgence, hypocrisy, wickedness and everything unclean.

By contrast He came from the Father full of grace and truth. He is described as being full of the Holy Spirit and full of the joy of the Holy Spirit. "For God was pleased to have all his fullness dwell in him." (Col. 1:19)

His purpose is that we should be holy, be like Him, full of the positive power and life of God. "From the fullness of his grace we have all received one blessing after another." (John 1:16) Jesus speaks the words His Father gives Him to speak so that "your joy may be full". He prays that His disciples may have "the full measure of my joy within them". (John 17:13)

Peter says: "Though you have not seen him, you love him; and even though you do not see him now, you believe in him and are filled with an inexpressible and glorious joy, for you are receiving the goal of your faith, the salvation of your souls." (1 Pet. 1:8–9) "His divine power has given us everything we need for life and godliness." (2 Pet. 1:3)

Paul prays that, "You may be filled to the measure of all the fullness of God." (Eph. 3:19) As members of the Body of Christ we are to become mature, "attaining to the whole measure of the fullness of Christ." (Eph. 4:13) "You have been given fullness in Christ" (Col. 2:9) – that is God's gift to you in Jesus.

And so when the disciples were searching for the right men to raise up in ministry, they were looking for those who were full. "Choose seven men from among you who are

known to be full of the Holy Spirit and wisdom." (Acts 6:3)
That is, they were looking for those filled with the positive,
filled with the holy fire of God's Spirit.

*You have been given fullness in Christ, who is the head over
every power and authority.*

4.   A HOLY PEOPLE

God is righteous. He is right in everything He does because He is right by nature. Whatever He does is just and right because He is the standard by which everything and everyone is judged. To agree with God is to be right: to disagree is to be unrighteous. That does not mean that we always understand His ways; sin and self-interest make it impossible for us to assess situations in the way He does.

Sin is unrighteousness, whatever is not right in God's sight. His just and righteous judgment on all sinners is that they deserve to die and be eternally separated from Him; they deserve the lake of fire rather than union with Him. That is not what He wants, but it is inevitable, because an unrighteous sinner cannot be in unity with a righteous God. He cannot say that sin does not matter as He knows its terrible consequences.

However, the Righteous God is also the God of love. The disobedience of the people caused His heart to be filled with pain. He is the Lord who has compassion and mercy.

His requirement for both Noah and Abraham was a blameless walk; not a STATE of holiness, but of a WALK of holiness, that both men exhibit loving obedience to God in their actions. Holiness is not a passive state but involves actively fulfilling the commands of God, doing what He wants done, and doing it in the way He desires.

The requirement to be righteous, blameless and holy was not solely for specific individuals. "You are to be my holy people," He tells the whole nation. "I am the Lord your God; consecrate yourselves and be holy, because I am holy . . . I am the Lord who brought you up out of Egypt to be your God; therefore be holy, because I am holy." (Lev. 11:44,45)

The word holy means literally "set apart". God desires a people who are "set apart" for Himself, His own people, His own possession, those willing to walk in His ways, who are faithful and lovingly obedient to Him.

Holiness implies, therefore, consecration on the part of the people: "Consecrate yourselves and be holy." They must be willing to set apart their lives for God, to yield themselves wholeheartedly to Him. He is not going to operate in their lives against their wills; He wants cooperation from them.

Giving yourself to the Lord implies a separation from what is unholy and ungodly. Turning to God involves turning away from sin. To centre your life upon pleasing Him means your life is no longer centred on self to please yourself.

Turning away from sin implies a moral purity and "purity" is a secondary meaning of the word "holy". God desires us to be holy, set-apart people, our hearts pure before Him and our lives blameless in His sight. He wants nothing less, and it is to this end that He leads every child of His. It was for this purpose that He was to send His Son to die on a cross.

In the Old Testament Law this purity was expressed in ritual acts, which represented the moral purity God was looking for in the hearts and lives of His people. They were to have nothing to do with practices, animals, food or people that were considered "unclean".

The punishments for contravening the laws of purity were dire because God wanted to see His moral purity reflected in His people. He wanted to demonstrate to other nations that His people loved Him and feared Him; that they were prepared to live according to His ways and so reap the reward of His love and bountiful provision. They were not to be corrupted by the ways of other nations, nor be led astray by their own desires: "You must not live according to the customs of the nations . . . I am the Lord your God, who has set you apart from the nations." (Lev. 20:23,24) "You are to be holy to me because I, the Lord, am holy, and I have set you apart from the nations to be my own." (Lev. 20:26)

WHO OWNS YOU?

The idea of God having a people of His own flows over from the Old Testament to the New: "You are not your own; you were bought with a price. Therefore honour God with your body." (1 Cor. 6:19–20) He sent His Son, Jesus, to make unrighteous sinners righteous, by shedding His blood on their behalf. There was nothing they could do to make themselves acceptable to Him. Jesus had to offer to His Father a holy and righteous life so that the sins of the people could be forgiven. With His blood all who have a living faith in Jesus are "bought" so that they may belong eternally to the Lord.

You cannot belong to God and claim that your life is your own. The ownership of your life has to be settled. Who is going to be Lord and to have the ultimate authority in your life?

The Father does not possess His children to manipulate them or cajole them into obedience. He values them, He treasures them. He has created them to be like Himself and to reflect His glory. "For you are a people holy to the Lord your God. Out of all the peoples on the face of the earth, the Lord has chosen you to be his treasured possession." (Deut. 14:2)

That was His estimation of Israel; how much more those who have been washed in the precious blood of His Son, and made His children. The rewards of obedience and willingness to walk in His holy ways are immense: "You have declared this day that the Lord is your God and that you will walk in his ways, that you will keep his decrees, commands and laws, and that you will obey him. And the Lord has declared this day that you are his people, his treasured possession as he promised, and that you are to keep all his commands. He has declared that he will set you in praise, fame and honour above all the nations he has made and that you will be a people holy to the Lord your God, as he promised." (Deut. 26:17–19)

Just as He chose Israel to be His own, so from the multitudes of those who cover the earth, He sovereignly chooses each child of God. Jesus reminded His disciples: "You did not choose me, but I chose you . . ." (John 15:16) Each of His children is to walk in the ways of Jesus. He wants you to declare today that "the Lord is your God and that you will walk in his ways . . . and that you will obey him." It is for this that He has chosen you.

In return, the Lord assures you that you are His treasured possession and He promises you will be "holy to the Lord your God". Because He has called you and set you apart as His own, He will fulfil His purpose in you; He will bring to completion what He has begun; you shall be holy, consecrated, set apart for God. Holiness is not what you do for God, but what He does in you.

Even if it seems there is very little consecration about your life at present, remember God has not finished with you yet! The more your life is freely given over into His hands, the more you will be able to enter into the glorious inheritance He has prepared for you. He promises His people abundant provision and blessing in return for their obedience. Can Christians today expect to walk in holy ways without such obedience? Are some in danger of looking for abundance and blessings without the holiness that God desires of His children? If they are, they contradict the teaching of both Old and New Testaments and cannot please God, for "without holiness no one will see the Lord." (Heb. 12:14)

Israel often strayed from God's ways. The Old Testament is an account of His remarkable patience and faithfulness towards His people, even when they were unfaithful and disobedient. Continually He has to call them back to Himself with fresh repentance for their sins and a willingness to make a renewed consecration of their lives to Him. "When you and your children return to the Lord your God and obey him with all your heart and with all your soul according to everything I commanded you today, then the Lord your God will restore your fortunes and have compassion on you." (Deut. 30:2–3)

He promises them prosperity and victory when they live as His holy people. What a joy to know that the promises of the New Covenant are even greater than those of the Old, that the holy and refining fire of God was coming to live among men to deliver them from darkness and bring them into His glorious light.

I am God Almighty; walk before me and be blameless.

5. LIGHT

Jesus came as light into the darkness of the world: "In him was life, and that life was the light of men. The light shines in the darkness, but the darkness has not understood it." (John 1:4–5)

Paul warns us that "the god of this age has blinded the minds of unbelievers." (2 Cor. 4:4) A man who is not alive spiritually lives in darkness and is unable to recognise the truth: "The man without the Spirit does not accept the things that come from the Spirit of God, for they are foolishness to him and he cannot understand them, because they are spiritually discerned." (1 Cor. 2:14)

The work of the Cross is foolish to him; he does not see his need of a Saviour. He cannot understand why the Son of God should come and die for him or how that death could revolutionise his life; "For the message of the cross is foolishness to those who are perishing, but to us who are being saved it is the power of God." (1 Cor. 1:18)

Only the Light of Jesus can penetrate spiritual darkness. Other faiths deepen the darkness while deceiving people by giving the impression they offer enlightenment. Israel was often upbraided by God for allowing their pure worship of Him to become contaminated by other religions. To turn to Jesus is not only to turn away from the darkness of sin to His Light; it is also to turn from other faiths that masquerade as light.

When the moral teaching of some other religions seems to coincide with some of the teaching of Jesus, we must not be deceived. He is the only way to holiness and only through Him can a man be made acceptable in God's sight. It does not matter how moral a man is, he cannot be morally correct enough to make himself righteous. Even the slightest of sins is darkness, makes him unworthy of God and puts him in need of being cleansed with the blood of Jesus.

Without that blood there can be no holiness, no matter how hard someone tries to please God, how determined he is to live a clean, moral, wholesome life.

It is Jesus who sits at God's right hand in the glory of heaven, not Mohammed, nor Buddha, nor Confucius. There is no Hindu deity there nor spiritualist, Mormon, Taoist, or Eastern Mystic. With Jesus are those who are alive in Him, those who are washed in His blood and who have lived in the holiness that He makes possible. To the Lord darkness is darkness and He alone is the Light of the World.

THE CHOICE

"The true light that gives light to every man was coming into the world." (John 1:9) The majority of those among whom Jesus lived did not understand what He said, nor believe in Him as the Messiah, God's Son. They were spiritually blind people who loved the darkness of sin and were wedded to the ways of the world. Even the majority of the religious leaders rejected Him because they were comfortable in their self-righteousness.

"He was in the world, and though the world was made through him, the world did not recognise him. He came to that which was his own, but his own did not receive him." (John 1:10–11) If men rejected the light they remained in their sins and self-righteousness, alienated from God and in danger of eternal separation from Him. "Whoever does not believe stands condemned already because he has not believed in the name of God's one and only Son," said Jesus. (John 3:18)

By contrast: "To all who received him, to those who believed in his name, he gave the right to become children of God." (John 1:12) Whoever believes in Him is not condemned. "I tell you the truth, whoever hears my word and believes in him who sent me has eternal life and will not

be condemned; he has crossed over from death to life."
(John 5:24)

It is not that God loves some and not others. "He died for
all." (2 Cor. 5:15) Potentially He made it possible for all
men to receive salvation. God's immense love for all
mankind is shown in the Cross. He "so loved THE
WORLD that he gave his one and only Son, that whoever
believes in him shall not perish but have eternal life. For
God did not send his Son into the world to condemn the
world, but to save the world through him." (John 3:16–17)

The great divide is between belief and unbelief in what
God has done for us in Jesus; between those who are
prepared to forsake their darkness and embrace the "Light
of the world", and those who want to hold on to the cover of
darkness to hide their shameful deeds. They reject the
Light as they prefer their own ways to the righteous and
holy ways of God. Jesus said: "This is the verdict: Light has
come into the world, but men loved darkness instead of
light because their deeds were evil. Everyone who does evil
hates the light, and will not come into the light for fear that
his deeds will be exposed. But whoever lives by the truth
comes into the light, so that it may be seen plainly what he
has done has been done through God." (John 3:19–21)

God wants us to experience more than a sudden flash of
light when we turn to Christ and ask for our sins to be
forgiven. Jesus is concerned that we "live by the truth",
that we walk in the light. Before coming to Christ we
belonged to the darkness and were children of the devil.
New birth means we belong now to the Kingdom of Light
and God is our Father: "I am the light of the world.
Whoever follows me will never walk in darkness, but will
have the light of life." (John 8:12)

Sin is darkness. The Christian is called to forsake the
darkness and walk in the light of God's love and truth, of
His righteousness and holiness. The man who walks in
darkness does not know where he is going and will inevitably stumble; whereas the one who follows Jesus walks in
the light as He is in the light. He lives as a son of light.

Do you want to live in light or darkness? Are you prepared for all the darkness to go from your life so that you can walk in the light and allow the light of Jesus to shine out of your life? Whatever does not agree with God is darkness – doubt, fear, sin, stubbornness, disobedience, pride, selfishness. Do you have any secrets that you try to keep hidden from others? Or have you allowed all the shameful things to be dealt with by Jesus' blood?

I am the light of the world. Whoever follows me will never walk in darkness, but will have the light of life.

WALKING IN THE LIGHT

It is not sufficient to say we believe that Jesus is the Light of the world, or that we have come to the light or even that the light of God has come into the darkness of our lives. He expects us to live in the light, to be filled with that light and to radiate Jesus in the darkness of this sinful world. "This is the message we have heard from him and declare to you: God is light; in him there is no darkness at all. If we claim we have fellowship with him yet walk in the darkness, we lie and do not live by the truth. But if we walk in the light, as he is in the light, we have fellowship with one another, and the blood of Jesus, his Son, purifies us from every sin." (1 John 1:5–7)

This epistle is one of the most challenging books of the Bible. In it John makes clear that we cannot divorce our relationships with one another from our relationship with God. The way we relate to Him is reflected in the way we relate to others. In other words, you can measure what your relationship with God is like by the way in which you relate to your fellow Christians. It is false to claim a relationship with God that is not reflected in your relationships with others.

If you are walking in the light with God, you will be prepared to walk in the light with others. Just as sin separates you from God, so it also sets up divisions between you and others. Light and darkness cannot coexist. Some have settled for twilight, a compromise between good and evil, righteousness and sin, obedience and disobedience. But neither Jesus nor John allows for such a middle state. They speak only in terms of light and darkness. The choice is between the two!

If we walk in the light we not only have fellowship with Jesus, we are also at one with all others who have elected to walk in the light. Then, John says, the blood of Jesus "purifies us from every sin".

This suggests we can only know complete cleansing by being in right relationship with others, by allowing God to deal with the fears, deceit, jealousies, resentments and other grievances that cause divisions between us.

Every detail of our hearts and lives is laid bare before God. His light can see all darkness, whether the sin is directly against Him or involves others also. He desires to see all the darkness chased from our lives so that we can know our unity with Him and with one another. He wants His blood to cleanse us from every sin.

This is good news because it means that the blood of Jesus has power to put right what often divides people. It is common, and very tempting, to make excuses for our breakdown in relationships with others. We claim it is a question of temperament, or the blame is with the other person. Sometimes reconciliation seems impossible.

Jesus did not die for our excuses – only for our sins. When we acknowledge sin to be sin, to be our fault and responsibility, then we can be cleansed of it when we bring it to Jesus. While we continue to excuse ourselves, the burden of guilt remains and the shadow over that particular relationship will persist.

For true reconciliation the sin on both sides needs to be acknowledged and humbly brought to the Cross. Mutual forgiveness of one another then becomes possible, not in a spirit of judgment or criticism, but in love, as both have tasted the grace and mercy of God. "Whoever loves his brother lives in the light, and there is nothing in him to make him stumble." (1 John 2:10)

There is no intermediary between light and darkness, or between love and hate. To love your brother is to walk in the light, reflecting the light and love of Jesus. "But whoever hates his brother is in darkness and walks around in the darkness; he does not know where he is going, because the darkness has blinded him." (1 John 2:11)

LIGHT ATTRACTS

To live in holiness is to live in love; it is not protecting ourselves from others, by withdrawing from relationships in an attempt to aspire towards personal perfection. Whatever is of value to God has to be worked out in relationship with others for Jesus wants us to be light in the world.

In the Sermon on the Mount, a sermon on practical holiness, Jesus says: "You are the light of the world. A city on a hill cannot be hidden. Neither do people light a lamp and put it under a bowl. Instead they put it on its stand, and it gives light to everyone in the house. In the same way, let your light shine before men, that they may see your good deeds and praise your Father in heaven." (Matt. 5:14–16)

If our lives are filled with the light of Jesus, He needs to be seen clearly in us by others. They need to be attracted to that light so they too will be determined to leave behind their love of spiritual darkness and will embrace the One who died to set them free from sin.

When Jesus met with Saul of Tarsus on the road to Damascus, He made it clear that from the beginning of his Christian experience this was his purpose: "I am sending you to open their eyes and turn them from darkness to light, and from the power of Satan to God, so that they may receive forgiveness of sins and a place among those who are sanctified by faith in me." (Acts 26:17–18)

It is the responsibility of all Christians to allow the light of Jesus to shine out of their lives as a witness to others. Our prayers for those living in darkness cannot be truly effective

if we are content to live in darkness ourselves. They will
have more integrity and power if we are walking in the light
of Jesus. "The prayer of a righteous man is powerful and
effective," James tells us. (5:16)

Jesus teaches us to pray: "Your kingdom come, your will
be done on earth as it is in heaven." We lack integrity if we
mean that we want His Kingly rule around us in the world,
but not in our own lives; if we want others to be doing God's
heavenly will, but are not too concerned about our own
disobedience.

REMOVE THE BARRIERS

To walk in the light means that there are no barriers
separating you from others. Do any such barriers of fear,
suspicion, resentment, judgment exist? If so they need to
be pulled down so that you can enjoy true fellowship with
others, sharing your new life, yourself even, with them.
"We loved you so much that we were delighted to share
with you not only the gospel of God but our lives as well,
because you had become so dear to us." (1 Thess. 2:8)

To walk in the light is to share yourself with others; that is
true fellowship. It is to share the truth about yourself, your
weakness, fears, needs, sins even. It is to share with others
the life of Jesus, learning to minister His power to each
other. To walk in the light is to live in love, willing to serve
others and give freely to them. It is to recognise that you are
not an isolated believer but a member of Christ's body,
living for the welfare of the other parts because you share
the same Head, Jesus Christ.

What walls or barriers have you erected between yourself and others? Are you willing to pull them down, to
confess your responsibility in having constructed those
walls? Do you want to share yourself with others, to love as
Jesus has loved you? He will forgive everything that hinders
that walk of love once you have faced those issues and
brought them to Him.

*If we walk in the light, as he is in the light, we have fellowship
with one another, and the blood of Jesus, his son, purifies us
from every sin.*

LIGHT FOR THE WORLD

Evangelism without holiness is reduced to a striving to
achieve ends without the proper means. We can engage in
schemes, crusades, missions, have house to house visita-
tions and see only limited fruit as a result, unless the
message is being lived by those who proclaim it. That is not
solely the responsibility of the preachers, but of all God's
people called to be His Body.

"You are the salt of the earth. But if the salt loses its
saltiness, how can it be made salty again? It is no longer
good for anything, except to be thrown out and trampled by
men." (Matt. 5:13) God wants His children to radiate His
holiness so that they will be effective in their evangelism in
the world.

"You are the light of the world," (v. 14) Jesus continues.
We like to think of Him as the Light, without seeing
ourselves in that role. There is no point in lamenting the
lack of light that radiates from us; better to allow our
darkness to be exposed to His light so we may be cleansed
of it. Light cannot shine out of fear, resentment, bitterness,
division, hatred, jealousy, anger, pride, selfishness or any
other sin. "For I tell you that unless your righteousness
surpasses that of the Pharisees and the teachers of the law,
you will certainly not enter the kingdom of heaven." (Matt.
5:20)

Righteousness to the Scribes and Pharisees was a matter
of being ritually clean according to their religious traditions. They were concerned with their appearance before
men, not with the spiritual condition of their hearts. Jesus
saw through their hypocrisy and exposed what was truly
going on in them. "Now then, you Pharisees clean the
outside of the cup and dish, but inside you are full of greed
and wickedness. You foolish people! Did not the one who

made the outside make the inside also?" (Luke 11: 39–40)

BECOMING A "LIGHTHOUSE"

The life of an unbeliever is like a house in total darkness. The Pharisees' attitude was to floodlight the outside of the building so that it had the appearance of light. That only intensifies the darkness of the windows, though, and makes the onlooker doubly conscious of the darkness within.

Jesus stands and knocks at the door of that house and waits for the response of faith, the invitation to come and take up residence. When that response is forthcoming, the door is opened and Jesus comes into the hallway. It is true to say that the Light has come into that man's life and if the door is left open, some of the light will immediately shine out into the surrounding darkness.

However, there are many rooms where the light has not yet penetrated, areas where there is no repentance and which are not fully yielded to the Lordship of Christ. The Holy Spirit progressively takes the believer around the rooms of that house, waiting patiently as each area of disobedience is pointed out. When the door of that particular room is thrown open by the Christian, the light of Jesus floods a further area of his life. Light can now shine out of the windows of that particular room where before only darkness was visible.

As the sanctifying work of the Spirit continues in his life, moving to one room after another, so light appears at more and more of the windows. The more light that radiates from the house, the greater the impact upon the surrounding darkness. It becomes uncomfortable for the unrepentant sinner to be too close to the believer; he feels his sin is exposed by the light that radiates from the Christian. He comes readily under conviction, whereas before he could successfully hide his sinfulness.

God does not want this to be a long, protracted business.

The more readily every room in the house is exposed to the light, the more readily the darkness disappears.

In times of revival so much of the light of God's holiness and righteousness is manifested among His people that sinners are more readily convicted of their sins and come to the Saviour seeking new life through Him. That is why God speaks to His people about holiness when He is preparing for times of revival.

EFFECTIVE EVANGELISM

To live in holiness and righteousness is not the most popular form of evangelism! The moral and spiritual state of society is a reflection of the moral and spiritual state of the Church within that society. Christians are called to be leaven in the lump, the salt of the earth, the light of the world.

If you have a complacent attitude towards sin in your own life, do not be surprised if others around you have a similar attitude, especially unconverted relatives and friends. Your prayer for them, let alone your witness, is undermined by that casual attitude.

The answer does not lie in religious practice and obedience to traditions. Like the Pharisees of old, it is easy for Christians today to appear righteous in their exercise of their religious duties and yet not radiate the life of Jesus. He says, "Be perfect," and obedience to that command has to begin by allowing Him to deal with our hearts.

"Do not judge, or you too will be judged. For in the same way you judge others, you will be judged, and with the measure you use, it will be measured to you." (Matt. 7:1–2) Our witness to others will not be fruitful if in our hearts we are judging them. Jesus did not come to judge but to save. He does not constantly criticise us for our sins; He extends His loving forgiveness to us. He died to deliver us from condemnation, not to make us think we belong on the scrap-heap. "Why do you look at the speck of sawdust in your brother's eye and pay no attention to the plank in your own eye? . . . You hypocrite, first take the plank out of your own eye, and then you will see clearly to remove the speck from your brother's eye." (Matt. 7:3,5)

If we are allowing the Lord to deal with us, then He will deal with others through us. How many ministers spend hours every week trying to sort out problems in others' lives, knowing that they are ministering out of their own spiritual poverty? Would it not be wiser to draw aside to seek God, for there to be a fresh dealing with Him, a new cleansing and anointing, a move forward in the life and power of the Spirit? Then he would be able to minister out of the vitality of what God was doing in him. Light would flow out of him and bring enlightenment to others. What a contrast to having to conceal your own spiritual dryness!

MADE USEABLE

It is not only ministers who need to heed this, for all Christians are called to be witnesses of Christ in the world. Many misunderstand and abuse what it means to speak the truth in love. They go to others and offload their criticism of them, adding: "Of course, I tell you this in love!" It would be better if they spoke of their own sin and need of forgiveness. To speak the truth in love is to encourage others, not devastate them. You are only to go to them in love and not with any judgmental attitudes.

In your life there are rooms that are still in darkness and Jesus wants to flood them with His light. He wants you to open the door to those particular areas to allow His purpose to be fulfilled in you. It is possible for you to resist Him but you hinder Him if you do. It may be that there are areas of hurt that are painful to open to the Lord or others. His touch will heal those hurts when you open them to Him.

The call of God on your life is to share in the task of spreading His Kingdom. There can be no valid excuse for non-participation in the mission of His Church.

An introspective Christian was given, through prayer, a

picture of a misshapen china teapot. "What can you do with such a pot?" he was asked. Obviously, it cannot be pushed back into shape; it would break. It could be considered useless and put to one side. Alternatively, you can use it for its intended purpose, even though it is misshapen.

That is a picture of your life. You are not yet perfectly what God wants you to be. There is no point in trying to push yourself back into shape, or thinking that He has called you to His service to work out in you a continual process of healing. He calls you to fulfil His purpose in your imperfect, misshapen state. As you obey Him He will reshape you and heal you. That is a process that happens as you serve others and give to them in the way the Lord asks of you. Meanwhile the holy fire of God will be at work within you to purge from your heart any darkness that prevents you from fulfilling your full potential in Jesus.

You are light for the world.

6. A PURE HEART

Some think the wrath of God is reserved for the Old Testament and passes out of existence in the New. Not so! Paul tells us: "The wrath of God is being revealed from heaven against all the godlessness and wickedness of man." (Rom. 1:18) Today He is judging and dealing with the nations in justice and truth, and yet what He is doing in the life of every individual is part of His grand overall design.

The blood of Jesus was shed first for the Father. It was the holy, righteous offering that He required to save us from the wrath that we deserve. He does not want to deal with us in anger, but in love, compassion and mercy. Jesus came to save, not condemn. He saves us from the wrath we deserve because of our sin and disobedience.

When men choose darkness rather than the light that God has provided, they place themselves in a perilous position. "Therefore God gave them over in the sinful desires of their hearts to sexual impurity for the degrading of their bodies with one another. They exchanged the truth of God for a lie, and worshipped and served created things rather than the Creator – who is forever praised. Amen." (Rom. 1:24–5)

The evidence of this is seen throughout modern society, people thinking they have the right to do with their bodies as they desire, fulfilling their cravings and lusts, worshipping the god of materialism. "God gave them over to shameful lusts," Paul continues. If people decide to live like that, He gives them the freedom to do so, but they will reap the eternal consequences. Even in this life they will never be satisfied or find peace. For to feed the desires of the flesh leads to the flesh demanding more and more. Give the flesh an inch and it will soon want a foot, a yard, a mile, even. "He gave them over to a depraved mind, to do what ought not to be done." (Rom. 1:28)

UNHEEDED WARNINGS

Warnings from God are as unheeded today as in Old Testament times; morality, let alone holiness, is considered out of fashion by many. "Although they know God's righteous decree that those who do such things deserve death, they not only continue to do these very things but also approve of those who practise them." (v. 32) Those words are as appropriate today as they were for first-century Rome. Paul immediately issues the warning: "You, therefore, have no excuse, you who pass judgment on someone else, for at whatever point you judge the other, you are condemning yourself, because you who pass judgment do the same things." (Rom. 2:1)

Perhaps many want to protest their innocence at this point, for conversion to Christ has led to a radical transformation in their lives. What Christian does not experience sinful desires? Jesus warns that it is the contemplation of the sin that is as bad in God's sight as the deed itself.

Under the old covenant it was wrong to murder. Jesus said: "I tell you that anyone who is angry with his brother will be subject to judgment." (Matt. 5:22)

Under the Law, God commanded, "Do not commit adultery." Jesus said: "I tell you that anyone who looks at a woman lustfully has already committed adultery with her in his heart." (v. 28)

In the Old Testament divorce was permissible because of the hardness of the people's hearts. But Jesus said: "Anyone who divorces his wife and marries another woman commits adultery against her. And if she divorces her husband and marries another man, she commits adultery." (Mark 10:11–12)

Vengeance has been the way for many since the time of Cain. Jesus says: "Do not resist an evil person. If someone

strikes you on the right cheek, turn to him the other also."
(Matt. 5:39) "Love your enemies and pray for those who
persecute you." (v. 44) Only in that way will we act as sons
of the heavenly Father.

BE PERFECT

The moral claims of God are greater in the New Testament
than in the Old, not less! He expects greater things of His
children because He makes it possible for them to walk in
holiness of life.

Paul tells the Ephesians: "For of this you can be sure: No
immoral, impure or greedy person – such a man is an
idolater – has any inheritance in the kingdom of Christ and
of God. Let no one deceive you with empty words, for
because of such things God's wrath comes on those who are
disobedient." (5:5–6)

Sin is rooted in the heart. Many who are not Christians
can desire to live moral lives; but that will not make them
sinless in God's sight. Only the blood of Jesus can effect
that. He does not wait until we reach a certain standard of
behaviour until He has anything to do with us. On the
contrary, He is willing to meet with the greatest of sinners
once they turn to Him, acknowledging their sinfulness and
their desire for new life through Jesus.

He does not set the moral standards of God before us and
tell us to obey them in our own strength. Because sin stems
from the heart, it is the heart with which He deals. If the
heart is right, the words and actions will also be right. Jesus
is always ready to meet with us whenever we turn to Him.

He says: "Be perfect, therefore, as your heavenly Father
is perfect." (Matt. 5:48) The word "perfect" here means to
be made complete, to become mature: the Amplified Bible
defines it as to "grow into complete maturity of godliness in
mind and character, having reached the proper height of
virtue and integrity".

Although God meets with us in whatever state of sinfulness we turn to Him, He then initiates within us a process of

growth towards that maturity in which we reflect more of Jesus. His holy fire not only cleanses away the sin but produces that refining work within the heart which results in the believer wanting to please the Lord by living in righteous ways, with right heart attitudes, desires and motives.

Your heavenly Father is not content with the fact that you are a Christian. He wants to see in you the desire for growth to maturity, that you may be "completed" or made perfect, even as He is perfect. He wants to see your heart open to His refining fire.

Be perfect, therefore, as your heavenly Father is perfect.

THE HEART

We are not acceptable to God in our naturally unholy, sinful and rebellious state. We cannot put holiness to one side as if it is only an appendage to the Christian life for particularly saintly people. We dare not shun the subject if it is at the heart of God's purpose for all His children.

It is possible to live as Christians and receive a measure of blessing from the Lord without ever aspiring to His best for us. In spiritual things the good is often the enemy of the best. The Psalmist asks: "Lord, who may dwell in your sanctuary? Who may live on your holy hill?" The Lord's answer is direct and practical: He whose walk is blameless, who does what is righteous, who speaks the truth from his heart, who does not wrong his neighbour, who fears the Lord and keeps His word. "He who does these things will never be shaken," He promises. (Ps. 15)

We are living in a time of shaking. Society is being shaken. The world's monetary system is in danger of collapse. Worldwide recession has led to millions in the industrial nations being unemployed. One country after another has experienced political chaos, coups or scandal. Violence is common in many of the world's major cities. The moral standards of society have become increasingly

lax and have compromised many of the major denomina-
tional Churches. The liberal theologians have done their
worst to undermine faith in the Word of God. Much in the
world and the Church is being shaken.

God allows the shaking, which may well increase in the
coming years. When things are shaken, the unshakeable
becomes more obvious. The one who stands on the Lord's
holy hill needs not fear the shaking. He is not content with a
doctrine of holiness; he wants to live the holy life that will
be pleasing to his Lord. He seeks to live a blameless life
before God and man, to do what is right in every situation.
He recognises the need for purity of heart, for that is the
source of his words and actions. He wants to encourage
others, not slander, judge, condemn or criticise them. He
hates what God hates, longing to have His view of sin and
His love of righteousness. He earnestly seeks the Lord and
is willing to be faithful to Him, even when that proves
costly. He wants the Lord to exercise His authority over his
finances, acknowledging that all that he is and has rightly
belongs to God.

Is this a description of the impossible? No, it is a sum-
mary of the holy and righteous life that God places within
the reach of every Christian. It is not a distant dream, but
the reality He desires for every one He has called and
chosen.

THE DESIRE TO SIN

However, every Christian has to face certain truths about
himself. Experiencing the new birth and a personal relationship with Jesus does not eradicate his desire to sin. He
still has selfish and ungodly desires which are a complete
contradiction to holiness. He may recognise that it is God's
purpose to make him holy, but that is a process which seems
very far from complete. Many of the sinful practices in
which he indulged himself in his former way of life may
have stopped; but some of the desires have lingered on. He
still reacts in proud and unloving ways towards others and

he still wants his own way. He may experience selfish desires of lust or greed that crave to be satisfied.

He discovers that he needs the Lord's forgiveness constantly, but feels defeated by the fact that he has to confess the same sins time and time again. He may believe that nothing can be done about this and takes comfort from the fact that God has accepted him as he is.

This is true; however it is not God's purpose to leave him as he is, but to change him into His likeness from one degree of glory to another. That transformation will hardly be noticeable until he has an earnest desire to be different, for God to deal with him and restore him to purity of heart. "Who may ascend the hill of the Lord? Who may stand in his holy place?" the Psalmist asks. "He who has clean hands and a pure heart." (Ps. 24:3–4)

Do you want God to purify your heart? Such purity cannot be attained by your own efforts.

We are totally dependent on Him to purify our hearts by the activity of His Spirit at work within us. Sin is deceptive by its very nature and our hearts are easily deceived. We need Him to show us our sins that we might repent of them; otherwise in our blindness we would miss much of what He sees all too clearly, and what He knows mars His image from being reflected in us.

REMOVING THE BLEMISHES

Imagine a landscape of fields and trees. Your eye is attracted by the way the different parts blend together; you are not conscious of the dirt that is visible in some parts of the scene. Now picture the same scene covered in snow. Many of the dirty areas are covered with a pure white blanket. However in a few places the dirt shows through and is immediately obvious because the snow has not covered those areas.

This is a picture of the old life and the new. Before you were a Christian the dirty, imperfect areas of your life were plainly visible to God and to other people. You chose to ignore the dirt and concentrate on what, to you, was attractive. When you became a Christian you were conscious of the need for those dirty areas to be cleansed and when you asked the Lord to forgive you it was as if a blanket of pure snow covered your sins. He brought about changes in your attitudes and desires; and yet some blemishes persisted, protruding through the snow, appearing more obvious than they were before.

You may choose to look away from those blemishes; but your eye is attracted back to them again and again. You can either accept them as part of the scene and know they will always mar the beauty of the snow-covered landscape, or you can ask the Lord to deal with them. He will do so, as soon as you truly want that.

The difficulty is that you may want to keep those blemishes, and that is why they persist. Even though you ask God to forgive you for them because you recognise they are sinful, that does not necessarily mean you want the root of those particular sins to be dealt with. And there may be plenty of blemishes in that landscape to which you are blind; you will not notice them until they are pointed out to you. Even then you may not accept they are blemishes. You may justify them by saying that they are an integral part of the overall scene.

God does not immediately convict us of every sin; many of the desires of the heart have yet to be refined, purified and changed. He deals with each of us step by step, purging us of one area of disobedience after another. Matters that at one time seemed minor and trivial concern us because we realise they grieve the Lord; they offend His holiness and righteousness. When we desire to have pure hearts we become increasingly alert to the dangers of temptation and sin.

A truth the Scriptures constantly point us to is this: if we set our hearts upon pleasing the Lord, He will keep us in His ways. When we sin, and we shall, we will be quick and ready to repent because the Holy Spirit will convict us of what displeases Him. Each failure will not produce condemnation, but a greater trust and dependence on Him and an increasing thankfulness for His love and mercy.

THE SECRET

The secret of holiness is to be concerned primarily not with your own unholiness, but with the holiness of God Himself. Holiness happens in our lives, not through a strenuous sifting out of sin, not by any self-awareness or introspective processes, but by looking away from ourselves to the One who is Himself holy, the One who has created us to be like Him. It is He who will point out the blemishes and create in us a desire to be rid of them. "Blessed is the man whose sin the Lord does not count against him and in whose spirit is found no deceit." (Ps. 32:2)

We only become like the one we look at. To look in upon ourselves will result in a constant sense of unworthiness and failure. With our eyes on Him, seeing who He is in His holiness, we shall grow into His likeness. Our desire for purity of heart will be intensified and satisfied. For He is a refining fire and as we look to Him He continues His refining purposes in us, changing us from one degree of glory to another.

Create in me a pure heart, O God, and renew a right spirit within me.

7. A NEW SPIRIT

When Israel obeyed the Law God had given, He caused the nation to prosper. He made a covenant with the people at the heart of which was the great promise: "I will be your God and you will be my people." A covenant is an agreement between two sides that is legally binding on both. The Lord did not have to bind Himself in this way; He chose to do so as an expression of His faithfulness for He was prepared to keep all the promises He made.

For their part, the children of Israel were to be faithful in obeying the commandments given them. The Lord caused them to prosper spiritually and materially when they did so. His blessings were poured on them in abundance; they defeated their enemies and enjoyed times of peacc. Again and again, however, those times of prosperity and peace led to disobedience and corruption.

The Lord raised up prophetic voices to warn His people; but they chose rather to listen to the false prophets whose basic philosophy was: "He is our God, so everything will be all right. There is no need to heed the warnings of these men. They speak as our enemies would speak."

The spiritual sensitivity of the people was dulled by their sin. It is not surprising that they disregarded the true words that God spoke through the prophets, because sin brings confusion into people's lives. When we sin we act as God's enemies and cannot hear His voice clearly.

The Lord warned His people that He would take harsh action against them to bring them back to repentance and His ways. But the increased intensity of these warnings only made the prophets' task more unpopular and often exceedingly dangerous.

When the Lord allowed their enemies to triumph over them, or famine to strike the land, the people would once more return to Him. Revival would take place and the Law would again become important to the people. This renewed obedience would enable the Lord to restore His blessings under the terms of the covenant, and once again the chosen people of God would prosper.

In their time of comfort and ease, the spiritual and moral laxity would soon return and the whole cycle of events would be repeated: God calling His people to repent, His call being rejected; God dealing harshly with them to bring them to their knees; repentance, revival, blessing and prosperity – and then the disobedience creeps in again.

The Lord was preparing for a better way. This cycle of events could not be repeated endlessly or He would never have a holy people for Himself. This only demonstrated that men were unable to sustain obedience to God's Law because they did not have hearts that were prepared to love Him more than themselves.

NEW HEARTS

Throughout the centuries of Old Testament history, God is preparing for the inauguration of a new covenant between Himself and His people. Under the terms of this new agreement He promises: "I will put my law in their minds and write it on their hearts. I will be their God, and they will be my people. No longer will a man teach his neighbour, or a man his brother, saying, 'Know the Lord,' because they will all know me, from the least of them to the greatest," declares the Lord. "For I will forgive their wickedness and will remember their sins no more." (Jer. 31:33–4)

This covenant will not be like the former one. That was persistently broken "though I was a husband to them". (v. 32) Under the terms of the new covenant the Law will not be written on stone tablets but on the hearts of His people. They will have a new motivation and desire to obey their God.

Through His prophet Ezekiel, He has a similar message: "I will judge you, each one according to his ways, declares the Sovereign Lord. Repent! Turn away from all your offences; then sin will not be your downfall. Rid yourselves of all the offences you have committed, and get a new heart and a new spirit." (Ezek. 18:30–1)

How could the people rid themselves of their sin and acquire new hearts? Only by turning to God so that He could do for them what they could not accomplish themselves. He promises: "I will sprinkle clean water on you, and you will be clean; I will cleanse you from all your impurities and from all your idols. I will give you a new heart and put a new spirit within you; I will remove from you your heart of stone and give you a heart of flesh. And I will put my Spirit in you and move you to follow my decrees and be careful to keep my laws. You will live in the land I gave your forefathers; you will be my people, and I will be your God." (Ezek. 36:25–8)

The Lord promises His people blessings and prosperity if they obey. And yet He says He is not doing all this for their sakes, but because He is determined to have a people for Himself, His own people, a holy people.

His purpose would never be accomplished unless He came to live in His people to enable them to walk in His ways. No amount of self-effort would do, for that self-life is corrupt by its very nature, bent upon pleasing self and inevitably displeasing God. "I will put my Spirit in you and you will live," He promises.

GOD WITHIN

This new covenant involving God living WITHIN His people could not be inaugurated until He had first come to live AMONG them to make atonement for their sins. The Word of God, spoken for centuries from heaven, heard clearly by the prophets but largely unheeded by the people, would be made flesh. Then it would be possible for all to hear clearly. Then all could know the Lord personally, as He had promised. With the cleansing of their sins they would be made acceptable to God and restored to fellowship with Him.

Then He could come and live within them by the power of His Holy Spirit. To enable them to walk along the Way of Holiness.

The Holy Spirit is God's own Spirit of holiness given to all true believers. The Spirit wants to keep you from disobedience, warns you against the spiritual and moral laxity that affected Israel. He is God living in you to express His life through you. To live in holiness is to allow the presence of God within you to radiate through you, through your character, actions, words, attitudes. He will produce the positive fruit God wants to see in you: "love, joy, peace, patience, kindness, goodness, faithfulness, gentleness and self-control." (Gal. 5:22–3)

You cannot walk in holiness unless you are cleansed from all that is unholy and filled with the Spirit of God's holiness. Only He makes it possible to live the life God wants you to live. Only by His work within you can you be changed into the likeness of Jesus. Only through allowing His life to flow through your life can you bear fruit and be kept from disobedience. The secret is this, "Christ in you, the hope of glory." (Col. 1:27)

The Holy Spirit is God's gift to you. Holiness is not you trying to make yourself a better person, but allowing God to live out His life in you. You have a new heart; that was His gift to you when you were born again. You no longer need to live to please yourself; you can live to please Him.

Your constant prayer needs to be that God will continue to fill you with His Holy Spirit so that His life will flow out of your life as rivers of living water; that your heart will be constantly turned towards His will and away from your own fleshly desires. God wants you to have a revived heart, a heart on fire with love for Him, so that you can bring revival to others.

I will put my Spirit within you and you shall live.

FULL TO OVERFLOWING

The Holy Spirit is God. He is not a blessing sent from God; He is God Himself living in Christians.

The Spirit descended on Jesus as a dove. In scripture He is described as the breath or wind of God; not a gentle breeze, but a mighty rushing wind. Jesus will baptise His followers "with the Holy Spirit and with fire," and He promises they will then be filled with power.

We see the wide scope of the Spirit's ministry by the way He is described. Life-giving breath, a mighty rushing wind, a purifying cleansing fire, divine power, dove-like peace – all are apt descriptions of His life and activity. He is the Spirit of love and joy; He is God.

The Spirit led Jesus and is to lead us too. The way along which the Spirit led Him was not easy and will not always be easy for us. We cannot live faithfully as men and women of God in a world opposed to His purposes and expect a quiet, easy life. The Spirit began by leading Jesus into the wilderness for a time of fasting and prayer, when He was tempted by the devil. There, the Spirit enabled Him to remain faithful to His calling and gave Him the Scriptures to address to Satan the tempter.

And Jesus promises that the Spirit will give us the words to speak when we have to give account of our faith to others; "for it will not be you speaking, but the Spirit of your Father speaking through you." (Matt. 10:20)

By the Spirit of God, Jesus drove out demons and brought the miraculous power of God into men's lives. Men could speak against Jesus, blaspheme His name and be forgiven. The only sin that would not be forgiven would be to speak against the Holy Spirit, or to blaspheme against Him – so precious to God is the activity of His holiness in the lives of His children.

BE FILLED

Those who imagine they can please God and be faithful to Him without having lives overflowing with the Holy Spirit only fool themselves and sadden the Lord. The man of God will embrace all of the grace, gifts, power and promises of the Spirit that the Word of God opens up for him.

How can we claim to be truly filled with the Holy Spirit unless He is seen to have a controlling influence in our lives? A man may be truly born again because he has faith in Jesus; but that does not necessarily mean that he has yielded his life to the controlling influence of the Spirit. He may want the activity of God to be limited in his life, so that he can remain his own boss.

Not that God takes us over and makes us robots. He wants to influence us and point us in the right direction, away from sin and towards the purposes of God, away from disobedience and towards obedience, away from unrighteous and unholy things, towards righteousness and holiness, away from ourselves towards having our eyes fixed on Jesus.

There is little point in claiming that a jug is full, if it is not. It may have a certain amount of liquid in it; there may have been a time when it was full to the brim or even overflowing. The pertinent question is whether it is full to overflowing NOW. That is God's purpose for your life.

He does not want you looking back wistfully to past times of blessing and anointing when you were conscious of being in the flow of God's activity. Are you full to overflowing NOW? Are there rivers of living water flowing from your innermost being NOW? Are others being blessed of the power of His presence in your life NOW?

You remove the lid first before filling a pot. If it is closed the liquid will only flow over the outside and make a mess. That lid represents self with all its sin and disobedience. God will not break through that lid; He will wait until you ask Him to remove it and genuinely want Him to fill you to overflowing with His Spirit.

You are incapable of removing the sin, the fear and doubt that make up that lid. These things can only be given to Him so that He may deal with them. Then He waits for you to yield the whole pot to Him. He cannot fill what is not given to Him.

When He fills you with His Spirit, He fills you with His holy presence. To live in holiness is now possible. He does not fill you so that the level of living water may slowly fall. He opens the life of His Spirit to you continually so that His anointing will be fresh in your life.

Even if the pot is full, the liquid cannot be used if the lid of self is slammed shut again. To live in continual repentance will keep the way open for the Spirit to flow in and the living water to flow out of your life. God's purpose in filling you is to make your life holy and fruitful.

"The Spirit of the Lord is upon me," Jesus said, "because he has anointed me to preach good news to the poor. He has sent me to proclaim freedom for the prisoners and recovery of sight for the blind, to release the oppressed, to proclaim the year of the Lord's favour." (Luke 4:18–19)

Because the sons of God are to continue the ministry of Jesus in the world today, He is ready to anoint, fill, baptise them in the Holy Spirit. The phraseology is not as important as the reality. It is not a matter of claiming to be filled with the Spirit, but of demonstrating the Spirit's life and activity INCREASINGLY in our lives.

Would any of us claim that our lives are so full of the Spirit there is no longer room for any of self to be manifested? Would any dare to say that they have no need of fresh anointing from God?

Do we have to keep on asking God to give the gift of His Spirit to us until He finally decides to do so? Not if He is the Father who gives good gifts to His children. Jesus recognises our need to go on asking for that fresh anointing and infilling with His Spirit. That in no way denies what God has already done in us or given to us. It speaks, rather, of that ongoing, progressive work that the Spirit does in our lives.

Just as we can never leave the Cross, so we can never

grow beyond the point of acknowledging our dependence on the Holy Spirit and our need for the fresh anointing that we need from Him.

The Pentecostal experience was not enough for the first disciples; God filled them AGAIN with the Holy Spirit a little later when they prayed, recognising their need for more of His activity in their ministries: "And they were all filled with the Holy Spirit and spoke the word of God boldly." (Acts 4:31)

To Jesus God gave the Spirit without limit (John 3:34), but He knows how limited is our capacity to receive and manifest all He is willing to give to us. His desires for us are boundless, but the Spirit will only be seen in our lives in relation to the way in which we are prepared to allow the Spirit to direct our lives.

He will baptise you with the Holy Spirit and with fire.

SWIM OR FLY

"His divine power has given us everything we need for life and godliness through our knowledge of him who called us by his own glory and goodness." (2 Pet. 1:3) If the Spirit lives in you, you have received everything you need for life and godliness! You are able to "participate in the divine nature", for you live in Christ and His Spirit lives in you.

Learning to trust the resources of the Holy Spirit is a difficult lesson for most Christians. We are so used to acting on our own initiative using our natural abilities that it takes time to learn how to respond to the Spirit's initiative and depend on His supernatural power. Every area of the Spirit's activity relates to holiness and we can become more like Jesus only by entering more fully into that activity.

You would not attempt to swim the Atlantic Ocean if asked to do so, no matter what incentives or rewards you were offered. The sheer impossibility of the task would be obvious. However, there would be no problem if you were to fly. You would only have to trust the airworthiness of the aeroplane.

To try to be holy in your own strength is like trying to swim the Atlantic. Allowing the Holy Spirit to operate in your life is like flying with you trusting in His power.

TRUSTING IN THE SPIRIT

Do you ever doubt? The Holy Spirit is the Spirit of truth. He reveals the truth of God's Word to you. He will "teach you all things and will remind you of everything I have said to you." (John 14:26) He does not speak for Himself, but only what He hears from the Father. He will reveal Jesus to you and make it possible for you to live in Him.

Do you need strength, guidance, someone to speak for you or pray for you? He is the Paraclete – the Comforter (who strengthens you), the Counsellor (who guides you), the Advocate (who speaks on your behalf), the Intercessor (who prays for you and in you to the Father). He will even reveal to you what is to come, giving you vision of the way in which the Lord wants to lead you to see His Word fulfilled in you.

After Pentecost when they received the Holy Spirit, Peter and the other disciples were transformed into men who were bold in ministry, and who could teach others because of the holiness of their own lives.

When Ananias and Sapphira tried to deceive them, Peter asked, "How is it that Satan has so filled your heart that you have lied to the Holy Spirit? . . . How could you agree to test the Spirit of the Lord?" (Acts 5:3,9) The offence was against the Holy Spirit and the whole Church was in awe of God's judgment on them.

Do you need more power in your life? And more wisdom? It was through the power of the Spirit that "the apostles performed many miraculous signs and wonders among the people," (5:12) and raised up others in ministry – men who were "full of the Holy Spirit and wisdom".

Stephen was such a man. Full of God's grace and power,

he did "great wonders and miraculous signs among the people." (Acts 6:8) Those who argued with him could not "stand up against his wisdom or the Spirit by which he spoke." (v. 10)

When making his defence to the Jewish Council, he called them, "Stiff-necked people". "You always resist the Spirit!" he charged them. And it was Stephen who "full of the Holy Spirit, looked up to heaven and saw the glory of God, and Jesus standing at the right hand of God." (Acts 7:55)

The Acts of the Apostles are really the acts of the Holy Spirit working through the apostles. The Spirit not only worked mightily through them but also came upon people to whom they proclaimed the Gospel. They dare not move without the Spirit's direction, or speak without His anointing. To do either would be to step out of holiness and into their own striving. "And the disciples were continually diffused (throughout their souls) with joy and the Holy Spirit." (Acts 13:52 Amplified)

Do you need more love, peace and power over sin? "God has poured out his love into our hearts by the Holy Spirit, whom he has given us," Paul affirms. (Rom. 5:5) "The mind controlled by the Spirit is life and peace." (Rom. 8:6) It is only by the Spirit that we can "put to death the misdeeds of the body". (v. 13) And if we are sons of God then we will be led by His Spirit. (v. 14)

Do you often feel weak and helpless, that things are beyond you? "The Spirit helps us in our weakness, intercedes for us with groans that words cannot express, according to God's will." (vv. 26,27) No wonder Paul says: "Be aglow and burning with the Spirit, serving the Lord." (Rom. 12:11 Amplified)

Do you feel depressed about lifeless worship and ungodly attitudes? The Kingdom of God to which we belong as Christians does not consist of religious, legalistic attitudes, but of "righteousness, peace and joy in the Holy Spirit, because anyone who serves Christ in this way is pleasing to God and approved of by men." (Rom. 14:17–18)

You cannot separate the righteousness that the Spirit desires to create in you from the joy and peace the believer wants to experience, or the signs and wonders you need to see. The Lord wants the total life and ministry of His Spirit to be evidenced in your life. "May the God of hope fill you with all joy and peace as you trust in him, so that you may overflow with hope by the power of the Holy Spirit." (Rom. 15:13)

Do you want a greater personal revelation of God and more power in your ministry? It is the Spirit, who "searches all things, even the deep things of God" and reveals them to us. (1 Cor. 2:10) It is the Spirit who is to anoint our preaching so that the Word comes "with a demonstration of the Spirit's power". (1 Cor. 2:4)

Do you need gifts of faith and healing, prophecy or tongues? God gives gifts of the Holy Spirit to His Church, ministries for building up the life of the Body of Christ, prayer and ministry gifts for the good of all. Through the life of every believer the Spirit wishes to manifest His life for the common good.

All these are aspects of the working of God's Holy Spirit and so must be regarded as part of the holiness that He is wanting to create in our lives. He wants us to be familiar with the use of the gifts that He has provided for us as ways of hearing His holy voice and releasing His holy activity in our midst. Just as Jesus frequently relied upon these gifts so will those who live in Him and desire to be like Him, not only in character, but also in activity.

OUR COMPETENCE FROM GOD

Do you feel inadequate to fulfil what God asks of you? Paul described the Corinthians as a "letter from Christ, the result of our ministry, written not with ink but with the Spirit of the living God, not on tablets of stone but on tablets of human hearts." (2 Cor. 3:3) He tells them, "Not that we are competent to claim anything for ourselves, but our competence comes from God. He has made us competent as ministers of a new covenant – not of the letter but of the Spirit; for the letter kills, but the Spirit gives life." (vv. 5–6)

Our competence comes from our trust in the life and power of the Holy Spirit given to us. When there is dependence on the Spirit there will be freedom, the glorious liberty of the sons of God. "And we, who with unveiled faces all reflect the Lord's glory, are being transformed into his likeness with ever-increasing glory, which comes from the Lord, who is the Spirit." (2 Cor. 3:18)

We are being transfigured into His very image by the Spirit of God working within us. So Paul says: "Live by the Spirit, and you will not gratify the desires of the sinful nature." (Gal. 5:16) "I pray that out of his glorious riches he may strengthen you with power through his Spirit in your inner being, so that Christ may dwell in your hearts through faith." (Eph. 3:16,17)

Understandably Paul urges the Ephesians not to "grieve the Holy Spirit of God, with whom you were sealed for the day of redemption." (Eph. 4:30) So they are to be rid of all that is unworthy of the Lord, all bitterness, rage and anger, brawling and slander, along with every form of malice. Instead they are to be kind and compassionate to one another, forgiving one another, just as in Christ God forgave them – to be imitators of God!

He urges them to go on being filled with the Spirit for they could not live up to such a high calling apart from Him. "For God did not call us to be impure, but to live a holy life. Therefore, he who rejects this instruction does not reject man but God, who gives you his Holy Spirit." (1 Thess. 4:7–8)

Are you going to swim or fly the Atlantic? Will you allow the Holy Spirit His rightful place in your life? God has given you everything you need for life and godliness. Trust Him to work in you.

"May God himself, the God of peace, sanctify you through and through. May your whole spirit, soul and body be kept blameless at the coming of our Lord Jesus Christ.

The one who calls you is faithful and he will do it." (1 Thess. 5:23-4)

He is Himself the refining fire – and He will refine you!

May God himself, the God of peace, sanctify you through and through.

8. MADE NEW

If we have been made righteous through the blood of Jesus, we are expected to live in righteous ways. "No one who is born of God will continue to sin, because God's seed remains in him; he cannot go on sinning, because he has been born of God." (1 John 3:9)

Part of the evidence of new birth is a determination to be done with sin and to live in ways that please the Lord. The Christian will feel uncomfortable about disobeying the Lord because His seed now lives in him. And the Spirit within the believer warns against sin, will convict him of sin and will cause him to feel uncomfortable with himself until he has made his peace with God.

It cannot be the nature of a true Christian, John is saying, to continue deliberately and habitually in sinful ways. "Anyone who does not do what is right is not a child of God; neither is anyone who does not love his brother." (v. 10)

To live in righteousness is not only a God-ward activity; it affects relationships with others. The believer is to be righteous in his attitude towards others, being loving, forgiving and merciful to them. That love is to be expressed in practical ways of caring, serving and encouraging them. "Dear children, let us not love with words or tongue but with actions and in truth." (v. 18)

True holiness is not being filled with pious attitudes, but is living like Jesus in practical ways, expressing the righteousness He gives us in righteous actions. If we walk with Jesus in obedience, then our hearts will not condemn us. Then we can have "confidence before God and receive from him anything we ask, because we obey his commands and do what pleases him." (v. 21–22) The rewards of living in holiness are immense. Jesus promised: "If you remain in me and my words remain in you, ask whatever you wish, and it will be given you." (John 15:7)

God wants us to have confidence before Him, to come boldly into His presence knowing that He holds nothing against us because we have been cleansed from sin and are not aware of any deliberate disobedience in our lives. If we have confidence in the presence of God we will be bold in what we ask Him to do. "The prayer of a righteous man is powerful and effective." (James 5:16) A righteous man is one who lives in righteousness; not one who is careless about his walk with the Lord.

THE CONFLICT

"Live by the Spirit, and you will not gratify the desires of the sinful nature. For the sinful nature desires what is contrary to the Spirit, and the Spirit what is contrary to the sinful nature. They are in conflict with each other, so that you do not do what you want." (Gal. 5:16–17)

Every Christian experiences conflict raging within him. Many are disturbed that there should be such conflict; but if there is no conflict it is likely they have yielded to sin. Your flesh will always be flesh and in opposition to God and, therefore, will want to oppose the working of His Holy Spirit in your life. If you obey the promptings of the flesh, your sinful self, you may do what your natural desires demand, but you will not fulfil what you want to do as a Christian, which is to please God.

By trusting to the power of the Spirit you are able to stand firm against fleshly desires and decide to please God by obeying Him. How can God produce His life in you if you still want to gratify the sinful desires of the flesh? They are crucified and need to be regarded as dead. If you believe you are still in bondage to your old nature you deny the truth and will experience an intensified conflict between sin and righteousness within you.

God's evaluation of that old nature was that it needed to be put to death. Jesus did not come to reform you; He came to make you a new person. There is no point in trying to improve the quality of your sinful self; that old nature was in opposition to the working of God's Spirit in your life and has been dead and buried with Christ. The conflict between the old and the new can only be resolved by constantly recognising yourself dead to that old nature. You do not have to allow that sinful self to be expressed any more. "For you died, and your life is now hidden with Christ in God." (Col. 3:3)

You are to live in Him, not in the past, no longer bound by those selfish desires and lusts. "Those who belong to Christ Jesus have crucified the sinful nature with its passions and desires." (Gal. 5:24) How can you do this? Wishing that these desires would go away does not work; they need to be taken to the Cross.

We desire what we want. If our desires are contrary to God's holy purpose we have to recognise that we want what He does not want for us. Those desires must be yielded to Him. Here is a simple way to do this.

DEAD WITH CHRIST

Draw apart to be with the Lord when you know that you will not be interrupted or hurried. As you pray, picture Jesus hanging on the Cross. Realise that He died there for you. Notice that He does not struggle to hold on to life, but quietly resigns Himself to His Father's will. (The soldiers were surprised that He died so quickly.) "It is finished," He cries. Everything for your salvation is now accomplished. He hangs limp on the Cross, His body lifeless.

You died with Him: "For we know that our old self was crucified with him." (Rom. 6:6) This is a truth that needs to become real in your experience. So now picture yourself hanging on that Cross. You are not putting yourself to death; you are watching what actually happened when you were crucified with Him.

Like Jesus you are stripped naked. Nothing can be hidden now, not even your secret desires. What are the issues that prevent you from being more like Jesus, those parts of you that are not consecrated and yielded to Him? Do not hold on to these aspects of self any longer. Don't try to bury them or hide them. Face them even if you experience struggle and turmoil as you realise that part of you wants to hold on to your selfish desires. When you have yielded them to God you stop struggling to hold on to YOUR life. Now you can watch yourself die. "It is finished."

You hang limp on the Cross. That old nature is dead. You are taken from the Cross and carried to your tomb, unable to resist. See yourself lying on the slab as cold and lifeless as the tomb. There is nothing you can do to raise yourself from that position.

Now see the risen Jesus enter that tomb. He takes hold of your hand and life enters your body – not the old life: His life. He lifts you to your feet and you follow Him out of the tomb into the brilliant sunlight. It is the same world that you died to; sin still abounds within it. But you are different, you are a new person and Jesus lives in you by the power of His Spirit. You are now able to resist the temptations of the world and can live the new life of Jesus.

Take your time as you relive what He did for you at Calvary and be sure that you face the necessary issues while you see yourself hanging on that Cross. You may need to revisit the Cross in this way from time to time as God confronts you with a further issue that needs to be dealt with. Or you can know by faith that when Jesus died on that Cross everything that belongs to your sinful nature died with Him.

Do not be surprised if there is still the temptation to sin in some particular way that you yielded to God. The world is still the same and Satan is very active in it. But every day you can reckon yourself dead to that sin. You can recall that you visited the Cross and saw yourself dead to that particular sin. You do not have to live in it any longer: "For we know that our old self was crucified with him so that the body of sin might be rendered powerless, that we should no longer be slaves to sin – because anyone who has died has been freed from sin." (Rom. 6:6–7)

You have presided at the funeral of your old life!

You died, and your life is now hidden with Christ in God.

DYING DAILY

You have been crucified with Christ; now you can live with Him. "Now if we died with Christ, we believe that we will also live with him." (Rom. 6:8)

Living with Jesus involves a daily dying to sin, deliberately turning away from what displeases Him and consciously giving yourself to Him to fulfil His purpose for you: "Count yourselves dead to sin but alive to God in Christ Jesus. Therefore do not let sin reign in your mortal body so that you obey its evil desires. Do not offer the parts of your body to sin, as instruments of wickedness, but rather offer yourselves to God, as those who have been brought from death to life; and offer the parts of your body to him as instruments of righteousness. For sin shall not be your master." (Rom. 6:11–14)

Paul makes it clear that evil desires still exist, but you do not need to obey them if you have died to them. Sin abounds everywhere but it shall not be your master if you yield yourself to God to live righteously. At any moment you can turn back to the old ways if you choose to do so. That is why it is so important that you keep your eyes fixed on Jesus and follow Him. "Live by the Spirit, and you will not gratify the desires of the sinful nature." (Gal. 5:16)

"Since we live by the Spirit, let us keep in step with the Spirit." (Gal. 5:25) Then He will produce His fruit in us: love, joy, peace, patience, kindness, goodness, faithfulness, gentleness and self-control. Such qualities are the very opposite to the fleshly desires we have which are centred on self-gratification.

"You have been set free from sin," Paul tells the Romans, "and have become slaves to righteousness." (6:18) In your old life your body was in slavery to impurity and wicked- ness, but now you are to offer yourself "in slavery to righteousness leading to holiness". (v. 19)

Again the apostle hammers home the truths so that his readers may live in the power of them: "Now that you have been set free from sin and have become slaves to God, the benefit you reap leads to holiness, and the result is eternal life." (v. 22)

`To become a slave to God and to righteousness is free- dom, not bondage. It is then you can know the glorious liberty of the sons of God. Because you have died with Christ you are "controlled not by the sinful nature but by the Spirit, if the Spirit of God lives in you." (Rom. 8:9)

When God forgives, He forgives and forgets. He will never look again on the sins we have confessed to Him, nor will He punish us for them. He will not allow them to affect the way He acts towards us; He treats us as if those sins had never happened.

Our part is to believe what Jesus has done for us. He wants us to know the joy and the freedom of complete forgiveness, so that He can take us on further in His purpose of salvation. "If anyone would come after me, he must deny himself and take up his cross and follow me. For whoever wants to save his life will lose it, but whoever loses his life for me will find it." (Matt. 16:24–5)

YOUR CROSS

The Cross of Jesus that brought us acceptance in God's sight was a once-for-all act, never to be repeated. The cross that each believer is to carry day by day, is not forced on him. It is the cross of self-denial, of preferring God and others before himself. It is the willingness to live for Jesus rather than for self: to obey Him, love Him, serve Him, honour Him and seek to glorify Him rather than himself.

In this life, you will never be free from temptation – the devil will make sure of that. And Satan will encourage you to act in self-dependence, to deny the resources of the Holy Spirit that are given to you, and will encourage that life of self which naturally lusts after the things this present world counts dear. "If you think you are standing firm, be careful that you don't fall! No temptation has seized you except what is common to man. And God is faithful; he will not let you be tempted beyond what you can bear. But when you are tempted, he will also provide a way out so that you can stand up under it." (1 Cor. 10:12–13)

TEMPTATION

The non-believer will want to excuse himself for his sins: "I couldn't help it," he will say. The Christian has no such excuse. We are only tempted where we are vulnerable, in ways we like to sin. We may cry out to God to take the temptation away; but it is not He who tempts us. "When tempted, no one should say, 'God is tempting me.' For God cannot be tempted by evil, nor does he tempt anyone; but each one is tempted when, by his own evil desire, he is dragged away and enticed." (James 1:13–14)

God cannot be tempted because there is nothing unholy, unrighteous or impure about Him. We are tempted in areas where our desires are not in tune with His, where we still want to please self rather than Him. To yield to the temptation is so much easier than to resist it. Disobedience is easier than obedience. But disobedience is sin and when we sin we lose peace with God until we are once again reconciled with Him through His forgiveness.

Why does the Lord allow us to be tempted? Surely it must be within His sovereign power to do away with temptation?

It is possible for Him to do so, but it is not His purpose. He allows us to be tempted so that we are kept aware of our weakness and vulnerability; so that we are conscious of the areas of our lives where the refining of God's Spirit still

needs to be at work within our hearts and lives, sifting out
the desires and attitudes that are opposed to His purposes.
Temptation causes us to look to the Lord for His grace to
keep us in His way.

Similarly, the Lord allows suffering in our lives to increase our faith in Him. Our faith would not need to be very
strong if everything in our Christian experience was comfortable and easy. We are told to rejoice in adversity and
suffering (not sickness!). He wants to use that suffering
positively. "We also rejoice in our sufferings, because we
know that suffering produces perseverance; perseverance,
character; and character, hope." (Rom. 5:3–4)

PERSEVERANCE

The character of Jesus will never be reproduced in us
without perseverance. We only have to look at His earthly
ministry to see how He maintained obedience to His Father
in the midst of continual opposition and difficulty. He was
misrepresented (and who of us enjoys that!), mistreated,
rejected, scourged, falsely accused and unjustly tried and
executed.

If the character of Jesus is to be seen in us in any
meaningful way, then we will need to learn to persevere
when we are confronted with opposition, rejection, misunderstanding; when great difficulties face us or traumatic
things happen to those around us.

Perseverance produces the character of Jesus in us. He
wants us to put our trust in Him in every situation, believing
that He will carry us through the seemingly impossible
difficulties, or even the niggling negative things that happen
from day to day.

Perseverance can only be produced by God allowing us
to be subjected to suffering. Even Jesus Himself "learned
obedience from what he suffered". Although as God's Son
He was perfect even in the days of His humanity, He had to
demonstrate that He was perfect; perfect in His obedience
when confronted with temptation or when faced with the

Cross, perfect in facing the various trials to which He was subjected. "Although he was a son, he learned obedience from what he suffered and, once made perfect, he became the source of eternal salvation for all who obey him." (Heb. 5:8–9)

The Bible teaches us to have a very positive attitude to suffering, to appreciate that "in all things God works for the good of those who love him, who have been called according to his purpose." (Rom. 8:28) That is a verse often quoted by Christians, usually in times of difficulty. But quoting it does not mean that a person believes it. It is one of those truths to which many pay lip service while disbelieving it deep in their hearts.

It is perplexing sometimes to know why God has allowed a particular difficulty to face us. It can even appear unjust to us that certain things are allowed to happen to us. We may experience considerable injustice in the world, but God will never deal unjustly with us. Coping with the world's injustice is part of the refining that is needed in our lives. We learn to persevere with faith in the justice of God, even when other people treat us unjustly. We do not have to fight for ourselves in such situations: God always vindicates His children when they hold fast to the truth. "Consider it pure joy, my brothers, whenever you face trials of many kinds, because you know that the testing of your faith develops perseverance. Perseverance must finish its work so that you may be mature and complete, not lacking anything." (James 1:2–4)

And remember Peter's words: "These have come so that your faith – of greater worth than gold, which perishes even though refined by fire – may be proved genuine and may result in praise, glory and honour when Jesus Christ is revealed." (1 Pet. 1:7) The faith God is giving you will never perish. It will be tested with fire, but will prove genuine.

If anyone would come after me, he must deny himself and take up his cross and follow me.

9. BROKEN

In recent years there has been a significant moving of the Holy Spirit in many lands. Love, joy, healing, gifts and many other blessings have been brought into people's lives. And yet in the great majority of places this "renewal" has fallen far short of the revival of former generations. For revivals have touched nations or areas in ways that renewal has not. Why?

Part of the answer is surely that people can be blessed without being broken. But they cannot come to holiness of life without brokenness. There is no revival without holiness and no holiness without brokenness. Jesus in His holiness manifested that humility of spirit: "Who being in very nature God, did not consider equality with God something to be grasped, but made himself nothing, taking the very nature of a servant . . . and became obedient to death – even death on a cross!" (Phil. 2:6,7,8)

The brokenness of Jesus was not the brokenness of sin, but of love and holiness. It is only through a "broken and contrite heart" that we can be brought to that same love and holiness. He does not despise those with such hearts because this brokenness is part of His own perfecting work within them.

A BROKEN AND CONTRITE HEART

Do you want to come to the point where you no longer shrug off your sins as if they do not matter, simply because you know you can presume upon the God of grace to forgive you? Can you pray that God will so deal with you that you will have a broken and contrite heart, that even the smallest of sins will offend you because you know it offends Him?

He will forgive you if you confess your sins to Him. He will extend His love, compassion and mercy to you. But is your love for Jesus such that you do not want to go on offending Him? Do you fear that He could take His presence from you if He dealt with you as you deserved? Would that be the worst possible thing that could happen to you? It is not His purpose to do that, but when we sin it often seems His presence has been withdrawn or that He has become remote.

God can use a variety of means to bring us to brokenness. One way is to be confronted with the awful nature of sin. This was David's experience: he had committed adultery and was responsible for murder. He turns back to the Lord in heart-felt repentance: "Have mercy on me, O God, according to your unfailing love; according to your great compassion blot out my transgressions. Wash away all my iniquity and cleanse me from my sin." (Ps. 51:1–2)

David realises that the fault lies within himself. He is bringing himself to the Lord, not only the specific sins of which he is guilty. HE needs to be cleansed. HE needs to be forgiven. HE needs to be restored to fellowship with God. HE needs to taste afresh His grace and mercy. "Have mercy on ME."

Because he recognises his sinful state before the sinless God, he wants all his iniquity and sin to be cleansed, not just the particular ones that had led to this time of repentance. "Wash away ALL my iniquity." Every trace of unholiness and ungodliness needed to be dealt with, for David realised that the real problem was the state of his own heart.

He had sinned because his heart was not right. If his love for the Lord had been what it should have been he would not have sinned in such serious ways. In fact, he would not want to sin at all. So he prays: "Surely you desire truth in the inner parts; you teach me wisdom in the inmost place." (Ps. 51:6)

He could not deceive the Lord. There was nothing that could be hidden from Him, even the secret desires and longings of his heart. It is in that innermost place that God wants His truth and wisdom to dwell. Understandably, David's request is: "Create in me a pure heart, O God, and renew a steadfast spirit within me. Do not cast me from your presence or take your Holy Spirit from me. Restore to me the joy of your salvation and grant me a willing spirit to sustain me." (vv. 10–12)

David is broken before God – and that is the way back into His holy presence. "The sacrifices of God are a broken spirit; a broken and contrite heart, O God, you will not despise." (Ps. 51:17) Thus speaks a man who KNOWS the Lord.

He longs to be restored in his relationship with the Lord, for then he will be a witness to other sinners who will see the benefit of turning to God in repentance. "Then I will teach transgressors your ways, and sinners will turn back to you." (v. 13)

The desire to sin comes from David's corrupt heart and puts him in danger of God's judgment. That would be no more than he deserved. "Do not cast me from your presence," he pleads, "or take your Holy Spirit from me."

Here is a man who has true consciousness of sin and the weight of it causes him to humble himself under the mighty hand of God. Do you have a similar consciousness of how awful your sin is before God? Do you realise that if God were to deal with you as you deserve He would reject you and withdraw from you? Thankfully, He deals with you with mercy and grace instead.

David knew the mercy, the great compassion, the unfailing love of God. He knew the power of the Lord to forgive sins and to restore him to grace. That is why he could pray: "Cleanse me . . . and I shall be clean; wash me, and I shall be whiter than snow . . . Restore to me the joy of your salvation." (vv. 7,12)

THE PRESUMPTION OF SIN

But he recognises also that he has presumed upon God; he has been disobedient and followed his own ways, fulfilling his own desires regardless of the Lord. Perhaps he forgot the Lord in the heat of his own passion; perhaps his attitude had been, "God will receive me back." Now, however, he is faced with the sin of his presumption. He feels he has slipped so far away from the Lord he fears losing His presence altogether and forever: "Restore to me the joy of your salvation." He has even lost the sense of knowing that he is kept in God's saving grace. Sin can have that effect.

Much of the sin in our lives does not seem serious enough to us to have such dire consequences. Yet we often wonder why the Lord's presence seems so remote and why the Christian life such a struggle. Like David, we need to come back to the Lord with renewed repentance. Dependence on the mercy of God is not to be confined to the initial stages of conversion. There is never a time in the life of a Christian when he does not need the grace and mercy of God to be extended towards him. Repentance is not an exercise for beginners, it is a way of life; not only turning to God but remaining turned to Him, being prepared to walk in His ways.

Ask the Lord to show you the sins that need to be confessed to Him, those things that are awful in His sight even though you may regard them in a casual way. Write them down. In that way you gain a truer perspective of what is really going on in your life. You can think of one sin after another without ever seeing the whole picture. When you see them all written down, you understand better what God sees in you at a single glance.

This is not an exercise of morbid introspection, but a way of bringing you to greater liberty. Bring all that is written to the Lord in prayer, ask Him to forgive you without making any excuses for yourself. And know that He promises to forgive all the sins you confess to Him. He makes you clean.

He is still merciful, compassionate and full of love for you.

A broken and contrite heart, O God, you will not despise.

BEWARE!

There have been men and women who have been mightily used by God, those through whom His Spirit obviously worked in power, but who have fallen into grave sin, pride and misuse of the ministries God has given them. The Lord continues to use them while giving them time to repent. If they refuse to do so, He simply removes the anointing. He does not withdraw His Spirit from the believer, but he or she is no longer anointed to minister in the powerful, effective way as before. God cannot be fooled and He will never allow His honour to be damaged. He raises men up and He lays them aside if their ministries become bigger than Him, or if sin and pride destroy the righteous relationship granted in Jesus.

We should be thankful that God deals with men in this way. It is a further incentive for us to walk in His ways, to persevere in faith, and not be sidetracked by our own desires. "Do not be deceived: God cannot be mocked. A man reaps what he sows." (Gal. 6:7)

It is sad that men are so easily deceived, but we are warned not to condemn those who fall into sin: "Brothers, if someone is caught in a sin, you who are spiritual should restore him gently. But watch yourself, or you also may be tempted." (Gal. 6:1)

The way of the Spirit is to make us increasingly humble before God so that more of His power and life may be seen in us. "If anyone thinks he is something when he is nothing, he deceives himself. Each one should test his own actions." (Gal. 6:3–4) As Jesus said: "The Spirit gives life; the flesh counts for nothing." (John 6:63)

The flesh in each one of us wants to deny vehemently that statement. We want to believe that we are worth something of ourselves and that the things we do by our own initiative and human resources are worth something to God. The man of God acknowledges that apart from Jesus he can do nothing; so he doesn't try. He knows that his flesh counts for nothing. He can only yield himself to God. He never ceases to marvel at the Lord's willingness to work through him. Not that he is seeking recognition for himself; he desires only that rivers of living water should flow from his innermost being, and that God would, therefore, cleanse from his life all that would hinder that flow.

HUMBLE YOURSELF

" 'God opposes the proud but gives grace to the humble.' Humble yourselves, therefore, under God's mighty hand, that he may lift you up in due time." (1 Pet. 5:5–6)

James quotes the same verse from Proverbs 3:34 and adds similar directions: " 'God opposes the proud but gives grace to the humble.' Submit yourselves, then, to God. Resist the devil, and he will flee from you. Come near to God and He will come near to you. Wash your hands, you sinners, and purify your hearts, you doubleminded. Grieve, mourn and wail. Change your laughter to mourning and your joy to gloom. Humble yourselves before the Lord, and he will lift you up." (James 4:6–10)

These letters are addressed to Christians; they are not evangelistic tracts aimed at the unconverted. When did you last hear a sermon telling you to "change your laughter to mourning and your joy to gloom" or to "grieve, mourn and wail"?

PRIDE

Pride holds many people back from committing their lives to Jesus and pride hinders every Christian. A stubborn refusal to hear what God is saying or to respond to His word is the result of pride. Every time we complain or argue with God, it is pride rearing its ugly head again. Criticism and judgment of others is another consequence of pride. All forms of selfishness come from pride. The fact that we dare to disobey God demonstrates that our hearts are proud.

"All a man's ways seem right to him but the Lord weighs the heart." (Prov. 21:2) He allows adverse circumstances so that our heart attitudes can be exposed and dealt with. He gives us difficult people to relate to and how often we seem to fail the test, asking Him to take the problems away rather than deal with us through them.

When we react negatively we demonstrate that we still have to be broken of pride over that particular issue or person. "The crucible for silver and the furnace for gold, but the Lord tests the heart." (Prov. 17:3)

He opposes the proud, and that includes the spiritually proud. No matter what God does for us, in us or through us, no matter how He uses us or how many others benefit from the ministries He gives us, ALL the glory belongs to Him. The work is not ours; it is Him working through us. Jesus tells us: "So you also, when you have done everything you were told to do, should say, 'We are unworthy servants; we have only done our duty.'" (Luke 17:10)

The humble man may know himself to be a highly privileged son of God; but he will never lose sight of the fact that, of himself, he is an unworthy servant, no matter how greatly the Lord uses him. Because God "opposes the proud but gives grace to the humble," he asks Him to reveal the areas of hidden pride to which he may be blind. He knows that pride will never be completely eradicated from his being until he passes into glory, but that does not lessen his desire to be rid of every attitude or motive that opposes God. And nothing opposes God more than pride. It easily leads to rebellion against His authority and lordship.

HUMILITY

Humility is the first sign of brokenness and is seen in a man's willingness to humble himself before the Lord. He can be open about his failures and sins; he can express

freely his constant need of God's mercy. But he does not
make a series of self-deprecating statements that only draw
attention to himself. His desire is to glorify Jesus. He
praises the Lord for His continual love, patience and grace.
He values highly the precious blood of the Saviour. He is
ever mindful of the condition of the lost and is faithful in
His prayer for them. "There, but for the grace of God go
I!"

Of himself, he is nothing – a worm and no man; but in
Christ he is accepted and highly valued by God. He realises, therefore, his responsibility to honour in thought,
word and deed the Lord he loves. His relationships with
others will be a reflection of his true relationship with God.

He looks for the best in others. He knows he is in no
position to judge, condemn or even criticise out of hand.
Because he lives every day at the Cross he is more concerned to pray for others than judge them. He will spend his
time speaking for them before the throne of grace, rather
than speaking about them behind their backs.

He is determined not to give the enemy any opportunity
to rejoice over him. Because he hates sin, he hates the one
who entices men to sin. So he will not allow him even minor
victories. Therefore, he obeys the constant urging of Scripture to be on the watch, to be vigilant and alert so that sin
does not overtake him unawares.

When he grieves the Lord, and it hurts him to see how
often that is, he knows what it is to "grieve, mourn and
wail" before Him. "Have mercy on me" is the cry of his
heart and he does not leave the place of prayer until he has
the assurance of forgiveness and has faced honestly his
need to be further changed by the Lord.

And yet he does not live under the burden of shame or
guilt; the blood of Jesus cleanses him from every sin. He
can walk in peace and joy, knowing the love of his Lord and
rejoicing to share that love with others, even in the most
humble acts of service.

He knows the walk of holiness is delicate; like a beautiful
flower its petals can easily be crushed or blown away. It is

that awareness that keeps him humble before the Lord, he understands the truth of His Word: "To the faithful you show yourself faithful, to the blameless you show yourself blameless, to the pure you show yourself pure, but to the crooked you show yourself shrewd. You save the humble but bring low those whose eyes are haughty." (Ps. 18: 25–27)

When you see such virtues in people, you can be sure they are men and women that have been dealt with by God. Have you ever wished for a similar humbleness of spirit? Do you fear that this would require cost? If so, you are right. It is only when broken of pride that you can know true humility before God and others.

YOUR FAITH PICTURE

Do not think that such humility is beyond you. Have a faith picture of yourself as the person God wants you to be and that you long to be. See yourself as that humble person. Imagine yourself reacting to situations and people in the way you should and not in stubborn pride or with anger, jealousy and selfishness. Then ask the Lord to deal with your proud heart. The changes He brings about in you will make the cost worthwhile. And as you grow in humility you will grow in confidence, not in yourself, but in the Lord who loves and encourages you.

Live with that faith picture of yourself becoming steadily more like Jesus. "Now faith is being sure of what we hope for and certain of what we do not see." (Heb. 11:1)

Do not be disillusioned when you fail to measure up to that faith picture. God is willing to forgive you for the sins you confess to Him. You need that faith goal to encourage you in your determination to please the Lord by becoming what He wants you to be. He will not give up on you but will bring you to the fulfilment of your faith picture.

And do not try to exalt yourself in other people's eyes to make yourself acceptable to them. You will not impress them with talk of your own godliness, usefulness or hard work. They will see more of Jesus in you when you act and react as He would. As the holy fire of God's love burns the pride out of your life you will be content to walk humbly before Him and before others.

God opposes the proud but gives grace to the humble.

10. THE WAY OF HOLINESS

Picture a narrow road raised above the ground on either side. The banks are steep and fall away to swamp-land where fierce animals prowl around. Because of the steep gradient they find it impossible to climb up on to the road. They can only hope that someone walking on that road will step over the edge, down the slippery bank and into the swamp within their reach.

Isaiah, chapter 35, speaks of the Way of Holiness that will be established by the Messiah: "And a highway will be there; it will be called the Way of Holiness. The unclean will not journey on it; it will be for those who walk in that Way; wicked fools will not go about on it. No lion will be there, nor will any ferocious beast get up on it; they will not be found there. But only the redeemed will walk there, and the ransomed of the Lord will return. They will enter Zion with singing; everlasting joy will crown their heads. Gladness and joy will overtake them, and sorrow and sighing will flee away." (Is. 35:8–10)

Jesus walked that Way of Holiness Himself; His entire earthly life and ministry is evidence of that. We must beware of trying to follow His example by our own efforts or striving. Jesus walked in holiness because His heart was right towards God and others. He wanted to remain holy and please His Father. Because His attitudes were right, His actions and words were right also. But if there is unholiness in our heart attitudes then no amount of self-effort will prevent that from becoming obvious. We will not want to be holy and will not be too concerned about displeasing the Lord. We will be in danger of slipping into the swamp within reach of the wild beasts.

We must want to walk on that Way of Holiness; to desire to meet with God, to know His cleansing, purging fire burning all the dross out of our lives that we may be refined like gold. But holiness is not a passive state, it is an active life that expresses godliness. Therefore, we have to face another crucial issue; whether we are prepared to walk with Jesus on that Way of Holiness, or not.

"The unclean will not journey on it." Only those washed in the blood of Jesus can journey along that way with Him. "Wicked fools will not go about on it." This is no place for those who love sin rather than righteousness, who flaunt their sin carelessly in the face of God, who live their lives for themselves and not for Him, or who are full of self-confidence.

Great promises are given to those who do walk this way with Jesus. "No lion will be there, nor will any ferocious beast get up on it; they will not be found there." Evil and good cannot walk together. Jesus in His holiness has overcome all the powers of unholiness.

THE OPPOSITION

The devil was a holy angel before he rebelled against the Lord by seeking to make himself the centre of attention instead of being content to worship the all-Holy One. There can be no place for rebellion in heaven and so he, and the other angels who followed him in disobedience, were immediately thrown out. "I saw Satan fall like lightning from heaven," Jesus said. (Luke 10:18) It has been the devil's intention ever since to cause men to fall with him, to lead them into unholy rebellion and disobedience.

Satan was utterly opposed to the ministry of Jesus. But he failed in his attempts to lure Him into acting on His own initiative when he tempted Him in the wilderness at the outset of His ministry. Although Jesus was tempted in every way just as we are, He never sinned. He never deviated from the Way of Holiness. The lions and ferocious beasts could not claim Him as their own.

When the powers of darkness thought they had defeated Him as He was led away to be crucified they failed to appreciate that they had only planned their own destruction. For the Son of God was to rise victorious from the grave. Not even death could hold Him. The Way of Holiness is an eternal Way that leads to eternal glory.

That is why the Lord encourages us to walk that way with Him. Yes, the powers of darkness will oppose us as they opposed Him, but they will not be able to reach us to snatch us from that way, so long as we are determined to walk on it. To walk in unholiness is to place ourselves within their reach. So James urges us: "Resist the devil, and he will flee from you." (James 4:7) And Peter warns us: "Be self-controlled and alert. Your enemy the devil prowls around like a roaring lion looking for someone to devour. Resist him, standing firm in the faith." (1 Pet. 5:8–9)

WALKING WITH JESUS

The redeemed will walk on that Way of Holiness, those who have come to Him to be cleansed by His blood; those who belong to the Lord, whom He is preparing for His glory in heaven. Holiness is a walk through life with Jesus, thinking, believing, speaking, behaving, praying, serving like He did. It is not simply the absence of the negatives of sin and failure. It is being clothed with Christ in order that we might live like Him.

When this Way of Holiness is established, "The eyes of the blind will be opened and the ears of the deaf unstopped. Then will the lame leap like a deer, and the tongue of the dumb shout for joy." (Is. 35:5,6)

Those words were fulfilled by Jesus in both a spiritual and literal sense. Through Him the spiritually blind have their eyes opened; deaf ears are opened to the Word of God. Those who have walked through life as spiritual cripples can walk in new life as new creatures, born again of water and the Spirit. And the spiritually dumb can speak of the One whom they have come to know; they can joyfully declare His promises and speak with thankfulness of all the Lord has done for them.

Also, the physically blind had their sight restored and the physically deaf their hearing healed. The power of the Gospel, and of the God of which it speaks, has not diminished over the centuries and He still works in the same powerful ways today. The lame are made to walk and the tongues of dumb people shout for joy.

Jesus has established the highway of holiness; He has made possible the salvation, the healing and wholeness of those who put their trust and confidence in Him. He demonstrates the limitless advantages and blessings that come to those who love Him. They can have faith that He will perform mighty works of healing in their lives for the glory of His name.

To those who are faithful in their walk on the Way of Holiness there is the promise that they will enter Zion with singing. They will know what it is to be liberated to praise God now, and they will join the heavenly host in their eternal praises: "Everlasting joy will crown their heads. Gladness and joy will overtake them, and sorrow and sighing will flee away." (Is. 35:10)

While sin persists in our lives, there will continue to be sorrow and sighing. While we are subjected to the temptations of the world, the flesh and the devil, there will be the constant need for vigilance lest we stumble on the way. But we are walking with the One who is able to keep us from falling. While we maintain faithfulness to Him we shall know His joy and gladness, even in the midst of trials and the tribulation Jesus says we will have in the world.

But when our earthly work is done, gladness and joy will overtake us completely and everlasting joy will crown our heads. "To him who is able to keep you from falling and to present you before his glorious presence without fault and with great joy – to the only God our Saviour be glory, majesty, power and authority, through Jesus Christ our Lord, before all ages, now and for evermore! Amen." (Jude 24–5)

To him who overcomes, I will give the right to sit with me on my throne, just as I overcame and sat down with my Father on his throne. (Rev. 3:21)

THE BASIC QUESTION

You will not want God's will unless you are clear about the ownership of your life. He has called you to be His child not for your purposes but for His.

The word of the Lord came to Jeremiah: "Before I formed you in the womb I knew you, before you were born I set you apart." (Jer. 1:5) Jeremiah was being called to a prophetic ministry, but the principle remains the same for every believer no matter the specific tasks God assigns him.

God was not calling Jeremiah to rejoice in his status, in the privileges of being one of His servants; He was facing him with the fact that He has chosen to set him apart for His own purposes.

The Lord knew you before you were born. He chose you to be His own: "For he chose us in Him before the creation of the world to be holy and blameless in His sight." (Eph. 1:4) That may not be the purpose you would choose for yourself; it is His will for you.

He has made you His child not for you to be satisfied with such status, but to be led by the Spirit, to recognise that you are totally and exclusively His, set apart to do His will, not your own. He has no lesser calling on any Christian's life: "You are not your own; you were bought at a price. Therefore honour God with your body." (1 Cor. 6:19–20)

THE OWNERSHIP OF YOUR LIFE

Many Christians have a constant struggle to face this basic truth about the ownership of their lives. Consequently, every time the Lord confronts them with something they do not want to do, they demur and a great debate goes on within them as to whether they will obey or not. Their spiritual lives seem to them to be a series of undesirable decisions as they yield themselves reluctantly to His will.

This situation is serious, for what is ultimately at stake is the whole matter of God's authority in their lives, whether Jesus is allowed to exercise His Lordship over them. They may call Him "Lord", but it is those who do God's will that will enter His Kingdom of glory.

This matter needs to be resolved immediately in your life. God has not called you to enjoy status but to live with the stature of one of His children. Every time He confronts you with something you don't want to do, He doesn't want a prolonged debate about it; He requires obedience.

The man who has come to full repentance has said "Yes" to the Lord, regardless of what the future holds for him. God does not give him a job description and ask whether he will be a disciple if the tasks seem agreeable to him. He calls him to follow Jesus unconditionally.

That is the commitment that is to be made at the BEGINNING of the Christian's experience. Sadly that does not always happen because of the way the Gospel is presented. People are often invited to come to Christ because of the benefits they will receive as a result. Those benefits certainly exist and are, in themselves, amazing; but they should not be the principal reason for giving ourselves to the Lord.

We come to Him for His sake first, that His purpose might be worked out in us, that we might do His will, not our own. Until that principle is clearly established, we will constantly be preferring our own wills to His. The purpose He has for us will be hindered again and again by our disobedience.

Because they have not yet faced this basic question of ownership, many ministers are unprepared to lead their people in obedience to God's Word and Spirit. They are afraid of people's reactions; their ears are more attuned to the opinions of men than the purposes of God. They are forever making excuses for themselves and the lack of vitality and reality of their congregations.

Likewise many lay people are not prepared to make their time and money available to the Lord in the way that He asks of them. They still want to control the day to day running of their lives. They openly say they are afraid to lose control of their lives. Jesus will not be truly their Lord until they do!

There is great security in knowing He is in charge. The man of faith is the one who acknowledges the Lord's authority. Jesus was astonished at the faith of a Roman centurion who recognised His authority. A Christian will have little true faith and authority in his life until he submits to the Lord's authority over him.

God has called you for His purposes, not for your own. Everything you are and have is His if you are truly His child. You have no rights of your own; you only have the rights He accords you as one with the privileged status of a son. He calls you to be holy and blameless in His sight, to be obedient to His Word and to desire His will.

If you have not already done so, sort this basic principle out with the Lord immediately. It is not a progressive decision that He asks of you. He wants you to respond to the fact that before the creation of the world He chose you to be His own. That cannot be understood with the mind, so there is no point in trying to do so.

The fact that God has predestined you in His love to be His child in no way diminishes your responsibility or hinders the exercise of your free will. That is demonstrated by the way in which you constantly have to make decisions as to whether you will obey God's Word, or not. Those decisions are infinitely easier to make once the basic premise of your life in Christ has been established. Like Jeremiah, you were known by the Lord before you were formed in the womb and He set you apart to be His own before you were born: "In him we were also chosen, having been predestined according to the plan of him who works

out everything in conformity with the purpose of his will."
(Eph. 1:11)

This does not mean that every decision God asks of you
will be easy. Jeremiah and many other men in the Scriptures felt overawed by the tasks given them. Nevertheless,
because he had the basis of his life correct, he consented
and did not refuse the Lord. When you agree that Jesus is
your Lord and that you will willingly and obediently serve
Him, no matter what He asks of you, then you will make
the right decisions, even if humanly you do not always want
them and they appear too difficult to face. Like Jesus, you
will pray, "not my will, but yours be done". (Luke 22:42)

Before you were born I set you apart.

11. FEAR NOT

Would it be loving for a father to allow his children to plan their own destruction without intervening and pointing out the dangers of what they are doing? Would he want them to indulge in practices that would damage their health?

Many parents have had to watch their children slide down the slippery slope of drug addiction or alcoholism, their every attempt to intervene resented and rejected. The heavenly Father wants to deliver His children from sin-addiction. He is prepared to deal with the root causes of sin in their lives so that they will no longer be addicted to self-pleasing unholiness. That is why He intervenes in our lives to point out our spiritual sickness.

MADE WHOLE

The English word "holy" comes from the same root as the word "whole". To be holy is to be made whole: health or wholeness of spirit, soul and body. Jesus took all unholiness upon Himself when He went to the Cross. He "took up our infirmities and carried our sorrows." (Is. 53:4) "He was pierced for our transgressions, he was crushed for our iniquities; the punishment that brought us peace was upon him and by his wounds we are healed." (v. 5)

God is concerned about the spiritual, mental, physical and moral wholeness of His children. The Holy One is not some vague moral force, but the God who has personality. He is the Father of His children and wants to be known by them through a loving relationship. He is, as Jesus called Him, the "Holy Father".

Many of the modern concepts of God's love are misconceived. He is often represented as indulgent of anything that would give pleasure or enjoyment to His people. But He alone knows the way to true health, wholeness and well-being. He knows that all unholiness is disease in His children. He regards unholiness much as we regard cancer, a dreadful disease that can eat its way through the human body causing pain and death.

To the Lord, unholiness is spiritual cancer that eats its way through the hearts and lives of His children. It causes untold spiritual and emotional pain and can lead to the ultimate death of eternal separation from God, for the unholy cannot be eternally made one with the Holy. This spiritual disease must be eradicated from their lives. No cost could be too high for that end to be achieved; His eternal purpose for His beloved ones depends upon it.

God's love can be clearly seen in His willingness to send His Holy Son to take all that He detests upon Himself. For when Jesus went to the Cross He carried on our behalf every vestige of unholiness, every sin, everything that His Father hates to see in the lives of His children. He suffered the rejection our unholiness deserves and that is expressed in His great cry, "My God, my God, why have you forsaken me?"

Those words reveal the total identification of Jesus with our sinful state, although He was Himself guilty of no sin. He bore our punishment so that, instead of the judgment and condemnation we deserve, we can receive forgiveness and His gift of eternal life. Instead of experiencing rejection by God because of our unholiness, we can be cleansed and made acceptable to Him. Then He can take positive steps to see that His holiness and love are seen in us in the way He desires. Then we will be whole, healthy people. ○

FEAR

Fear causes many Christians considerable dis-ease because it is sin. This is not always recognised. Some seek ministry, deliverance or healing for their fears, when what is truly needed first is repentance.

The perfect love of God casts out all fear. He wants to remove terror from their lives. He does not desire them to live in fear of men, nor to fear the consequences of obeying Him. There is a right fear of God, being in awe of Him and fearing to disobey Him. But His children need never fear coming to Him, for He will always meet them with love and compassion, with mercy and forgiveness. "If we claim to be without sin, we deceive ourselves and the truth is not in us. If we confess our sins, he is faithful and just and will forgive us our sins and purify us from all unrighteousness." (1 John 1:8–9)

The Lord does not condemn us for our unrighteousness; He forgives us because Jesus has offered His righteous life on our behalf. It is His purpose to "purify us from all unrighteousness", to cleanse out of our lives everything that is not right. If we refuse to come to Him to be cleansed, we place ourselves in condemnation, and condemnation produces fear.

Most people think of fear as an absence of faith, a total lack of confidence. In fact fear is the result of confidence that is misplaced. A person need only fear if his confidence is in himself. No one will be afraid if his confidence is in the love of Jesus, no matter how traumatic his circumstances. His heart and mind will be kept in the peace that is beyond understanding.

Fearful people seem to have little or no confidence and usually think and speak about themselves in negative terms. In fact, such people are full of self-confidence.

The quiet, introverted, negative person radiates little faith in Jesus because his confidence is in himself. He realises that his "self" life is not worth much; so he feels doomed to constant failure. He may pray to be set free from his fears and quote incessantly the Scripture that "perfect love casts out all fear"; but still there will be little change in his life. He will be fighting continually the negative fears and feelings which seem to dominate him.

At first he might not believe his real problem is self-confidence as that is the very thing he apparently lacks, has always longed for and has envied in others. Yet he cannot understand why the Lord should leave him dominated by so much fear. He may have cried out many times for God to free him from fear and sought ministry from others to set him free, all to little avail.

He fears because he trusts in himself with all his imperfections and weaknesses. The Lord will deliver him from fear when he comes to the Cross and confesses the sin of his self-confidence; that all these years past he has trusted in himself, in his flesh, and not in the Lord. Then he will be free to entrust himself with greater confidence in the Lord.

If you saw a notice "DANGER! THIN ICE" you would be foolish to venture on to it. Yet many people recognise how weak they are and still stand on that thin ice instead of the rock of Jesus. Is it any wonder that they feel the ground is always giving way beneath them?

It makes no sense to recognise what weak, sinful failures we are and to trust ourselves, believe our feelings and try to accomplish things by our own efforts. If we admit the total inadequacy of the self-life, we can throw ourselves on God's mercy. However, it cannot be emphasised enough how important it is to recognise that the real problem that needs to be confessed is not the weakness itself, but our self-confidence although we are so weak.

The more extrovert person has the same problem in a totally different guise. His confidence is in his abilities, rather than in his weakness. That is equally confidence in the flesh and means nothing to God. As the negative self-confidence has to come to the Cross, so does that proud self-assurance. Neither have any place before the throne of God and both need to be cleansed by the blood of Jesus.

THE END OF SELF-CONFIDENCE

Your faith and confidence in the Lord will never be strong until you are ready to come to the end of your self-confidence, whether of the negative or self-assured variety. Then you will be prepared to humble yourself before God and confess the pride, sin and folly of trusting yourself.

Even the person who suffers from the negative self-assurance is guilty of deep pride. He may appear to be humble and self-effacing, but it is pride to trust in himself rather than in the Lord. Negative people feel utterly useless because they have not recognised the deep pride that exists in believing their own negativity rather than the Lord of life.

Some will claim that they feel unable to believe and trust Him. That is only because they have not seen the nature of their pride and repented of it. Beyond the Cross there is liberty. There is no condemnation for those who belong to Jesus Christ.

He has come to save us: from sin, unrighteousness, disobedience, ungodliness, unholiness, the powers of evil and disease – and from the pride of self-confidence, self-assurance and self-dependence. Our eyes need to be opened to the nature of the pride that afflicts us all so that we may be delivered from it by Jesus.

His answer to fear was not analysis and endless ministry, but a simple command repeated over and over again to impress His disciples with its truth: "Fear not." That sounds too simplistic for our modern society with all its psychological awareness. But Jesus knew what He was talking about.

His commands are neither burdensome nor impossible to keep. There is no need to fear because Jesus is with you always. If you are trusting in yourself, you are guilty of self-confidence and will not be trusting in His presence. Is it any wonder that you fear if that is the case? He tells you not to fear because His Father has chosen to give you the Kingdom of God; all the resources of heaven are available to you.

You do not need to be anxious about tomorrow, or about what to eat or wear, if you are seeking first the Kingdom of God and His righteousness. All these things, Jesus promises, will be given to you. He will meet your every need according to His glorious riches.

If your confidence is in Jesus you will not fear. Even in danger the Lord rebuked His disciples for their unbelief: "Why are you so afraid? Do you still have no faith?" (Mark 4:40) In one situation after another He encouraged people not to be afraid: "Don't be afraid; just believe." (Mark 5:36)

Just as fear is the result of self-confidence, so faith comes from confidence in Jesus. If your faith is in Him and His Word, you will not have to fear men, need, circumstances, the future, or death even. If you trust in all Jesus has done for you on the Cross you will come to the Father, cleansed from fear and self-confidence by His blood, with full assurance of faith. You will be assured of His love for you and His perfect love, expressed in His forgiveness, has set you free from fear. That will be a significant part of the total healing that God wants to do in your life. When you are no longer bound by irrational fears and negative thinking you will be a more "whole" or "holy" person, able to reflect Jesus more fully.

Does this mean that nobody can be bound by fear? Not at all! Many of the world's religions, the occult and much spiritism is based on fear, thus revealing their satanic origins. It is often necessary to pray with those who have worshipped other spirits to be delivered from the fear these spirits have inflicted upon them. When a person turns to Christ, it is essential that he turns away from everything false: all fortune-telling, clairvoyance and superstition; that he destroys all fetishes and charms; that he renounces every association with the occult, freemasonry, yoga and martial arts and every other activity that is associated with the demonic.

People often experience irrational fears and bondages without realising their satanic origins. There is no need for the Christian to fear remaining in any such bondage. The power of the name and the blood of Jesus is greater than any other force or spiritual power. Once those are renounced, the believer is easily set free from all their influences.

Our confidence is not to be in ourselves, neither are we to fear the enemy, who is already crushed beneath the feet of Jesus and is to be crushed beneath our feet too.

Certainly we will not be afraid if we learn to live in the power of God's Word, believing the revelation He gives us of the victory that is already ours through Jesus.

Don't be afraid; just believe.

12. ACCORDING TO YOUR WORD

The changes God desires to bring about in our lives, individually and corporately, are radical. "The Spirit gives life; the flesh counts for nothing. The words I have spoken to you are spirit and they are life." (John 6:63)

To live in holiness is to live to fulfil the Word of God in your life. "If you hold to my teaching, you are really my disciples. Then you will know the truth, and the truth will set you free." (John 8:31–32) God's truth brings liberty into our lives. His Word shows us the way to be free of sin, fear and doubt; His Word conveys forgiveness, deliverance and healing to us. That Word shows us the way in which we are to walk as His holy people. "The entrance of your words gives light." (Ps. 119:130)

In that psalm the writer asks: "How can a young man keep his way pure?" He answers the question by saying: "By living according to your word. I seek you with all my heart; do not let me stray from your commands. I have hidden your word in my heart that I might not sin against you." (Ps. 119:9–11) He tells the Lord to "renew my life according to your word". (v. 25) He prays: "Turn my heart towards your statutes and not towards selfish gain. Turn my eyes away from worthless things; renew my life according to your word." (vv. 36–7)

"Renew my life in your righteousness." (v. 40) He can say: "You are my portion, O Lord; I have promised to obey your words. I have sought your face with all my heart." (vv. 57–8) He recognises: "I gain understanding from your precepts; therefore I hate every wrong path." (v. 104) Therefore: "Your word is a lamp to my feet and a light for my path." (v. 105)

How can we tell what is holy and unholy? Certainly not by our feelings; they will be a most unreliable indicator. It is easy to drown the inner witness or voice of the Spirit, especially when our emotions are involved. If we allow our feelings to govern our wills then we will fall into sin time and time again, and then experience the deep remorse of knowing we grieved God, not only by the sinful act but by failing to heed His gentle, but persistent, warnings.

As we read the Scriptures we see clearly what God expects of His children. The teaching of Jesus is direct and simple in this matter of holiness. In a real sense, all His teaching relates to this subject. But He gives clear direction as to how we are to live and relate to one another, how we are to speak, to believe, to think and what attitudes there need to be in our hearts.

THE WORD IS PRACTICAL AND POWERFUL

Such practical teaching is found throughout the New Testament. Even Paul, after brilliant and profound exposition of Christian doctrine, follows such teaching with clear practical direction as to what it means for that doctrine to be lived out in the lives of believers. For example, there is no greater statement of what God has accomplished for us in Jesus than the opening chapters of Ephesians. In chapter 4, however, he tells his readers what it means to live as children of light. He begins the following chapter by saying, "Be imitators of God," and goes on to give specific instruction to wives, husbands, children, slaves and masters.

The New Testament is not a book of spiritual theory; it is intensely practical. If you want to know how much of God's holiness is actually being expressed in your life, you only have to turn to the Scriptures and ask yourself whether you are living what is taught there.

Because the Word of God contains the power of God, it contains the power to make us holy: to show us how to stand firm against temptation, be dead to the old life of self, to avail ourselves of the spiritual resources He makes available to us and be filled with the Spirit. The Father sanctifies us by revealing the truth of His Word to our hearts.

God's Word is not too hard for you to face: "Now what I am commanding you today is not too difficult for you or beyond your reach. It is not up in heaven, so that you have to ask, 'Who will ascend into heaven to get it and proclaim it to us so that we may obey it?' Nor is it beyond the sea, so that you have to ask, 'Who will cross the sea to get it and proclaim it to us so that we may obey it?' No, the word is very near you; it is in your mouth and in your heart so that you may obey it." (Deut. 30:11–14)

The Lord brings His Word near to us and places it in our hearts by the Holy Spirit. He enables us to speak it and perform it by the grace of His Spirit working in us: "See, I set before you today life and prosperity, death and destruction. For I command you today to love the Lord your God, to walk in His ways, and to keep His commands, decrees and laws; then you will live and increase, and the Lord your God will bless you in the land you are entering to possess." (Deut. 30:15–16)

THE LORD IS YOUR LIFE

He lays clearly before the people the choice that confronts them: the broad way that leads to destruction, or the narrow way that leads to eternal life: "I have set before you life and death, blessings and curses. Now choose life, so that you and your children may live and that you may love the Lord your God, listen to His voice, and hold fast to him. For the Lord is your life." (vv. 19–20)

This is the essence of the Christian life: "The Lord is your life." He is not a part of your life; He IS your life. He is not someone simply to acknowledge as one who takes an interest in you. He is your life. He is more than a God of love who wants to bless you. He is your life.

If we acknowledge that truth we do not need to linger over the warnings the Lord gives to the disobedient. The

Lord spoke these words in the context of the Israelites needing to cross the Jordan to possess the Promised Land. Christians who want to please God by living His ways are faced with a similar radical decision. It will involve yielding the very parts of their lives they have so far managed successfully to keep from His control. It will mean stepping out in faith in ways that may be challenging. It may mean a change of lifestyle that others will misunderstand or even ridicule.

However, it is not true to plead: "I can't, Lord." His answer is simple: "Now what I am commanding you today is not too difficult for you or beyond your reach." If you have a will to walk in the Lord's way of holiness, He certainly will walk with you. The alternative? "For when I called, no one answered, when I spoke, no one listened. They did evil in my sight and chose what displeases me." (Is. 66:4)

The demands of the Holy God upon His children are total. They are to love Him with ALL their hearts, souls, minds and strength. He is to be their life, no matter what their occupation or social standing. To be a child of God is to be one of His holy people, set apart to live totally for Him. "This is the one I esteem: he who is humble and contrite in spirit, and trembles at my word." (Is. 66:2)

WORDS OF LIFE AND HEALING

Sometimes there is the temptation to "verse-hop". You can be reading a passage of Scripture and suddenly come across a verse that seems too hard to face in its implications. Perhaps that particular verse speaks to your heart about correction or discipline that you need. How tempting to hop over that verse and search for something more appealing and faith-building!

We need all the Scriptures, especially those verses God is applying to our hearts. We must not lose sight of them, even if they are uncomfortable. Such verses will cease to be uncomfortable as soon as you have responded to what God is saying. That verse will no longer be a threat but a means of blessing, for God will have used it to bring you to a new place of obedience.

Such words bring healing into our lives, His salvation, wholeness and holiness. Without His Word we would not know what holiness involves nor would we be aware of the means that God has provided to bring us into His holiness. "My son, pay attention to what I say; listen closely to my words. Do not let them out of your sight, keep them within your heart; for they are life to those who find them and health to a man's whole body. Above all else, guard your heart, for it is the wellspring of life." (Prov. 4:20–23)

If His words are grafted into our hearts we will be concerned to live them, not merely listen to them. And your heart is the "wellspring of life". From your heart will flow the living water of the Spirit. But if we do not allow God to deal with the impurities in our hearts then we see a mixture flowing out: something of the Spirit and still too much of us. "The Lord detests men of perverse heart but he delights in those whose ways are blameless." (Prov. 11:20)

Are you a man or woman of the Word? Do you come eagerly to the Scriptures believing God wants to speak words of revelation to your heart, to build and encourage you in faith? Do you allow Him to correct you through His Word, showing you how your life does not correspond with His wishes?

You will need to feed in the Scriptures daily if you are to walk as Jesus did – not because you try to imitate His actions, but because the Word brings you the light of God's truth about Him, His purpose and about you. Do not avoid the words of God; realise they are given you to be life, light and healing.

If you want to listen to the radio you don't switch if off. If you are seeking direction from someone, you don't close your ears to what he says. If you want to honour God in your life, you don't neglect His Word. You read it, listen to it, study it, obey it and live it. And you will find that, even when He corrects you, the Lord will always encourage you and assure you of His love. For faith comes from hearing those words spoken to your heart.

"Let the one who has my word speak it faithfully . . . Is not my word like fire," declares the Lord, "and like a hammer that breaks a rock in pieces?" (Jer. 23:28–9) There is no situation too powerful, no problem too great, no need too desperate, no bondage too heavy to be dealt with by hearing God speak His Word to your heart. That is how so much of the negative is removed from our lives. When we respond positively to what He says, the Word becomes as fire that purges, cleanses, delivers and heals!

The Spirit gives life; the flesh counts for nothing. The words I have spoken to you are spirit and they are life.

13. HOLY LORD

Our ability to believe in the truth of His Word and in the promises that He gives, is dependent upon our personal encounter with the Lord Himself. In the same way our growth in holiness is deeply affected by our personal experience of God in His holiness. Such encounters are at the same time both wonderful and disarming. Isaiah testifies: "I saw the Lord seated on a throne, high and exalted, and the train of his robe filled the temple." (Is. 6:1)

God's majesty cannot be separated from His holiness, or His holiness from His love. He is the Lord reigning in glory, the Holy One, who is Love. He is Righteous in His being and therefore in His ways. He is just by nature and therefore just in His dealings with men. He is Faith, Truth, Light – and much more besides.

The heavenly beings Isaiah saw surrounding the Lord in His glory "were calling to one another: 'Holy, holy, holy is the Lord Almighty; the whole earth is full of his glory.'" (Is. 6:3) They were proclaiming that He is completely beyond all He has made, is sufficient in Himself and is worthy of worship from all He has made in heaven or on earth.

St John's vision of heaven, described in detail in the Book of Revelation, endorses this. There the creatures surrounding God's throne never stop saying day and night: "Holy, holy, holy is the Lord God Almighty, who was, and is, and is to come." (Rev. 4:8)

Such experiences, whether given to an Isaiah or a John, or to anybody else, can only be partial, momentary glimpses of the Lord in His majestic and glorious holiness. This is all man could bear in his earthly state. When we see Him as

He is we shall be like Him, for the work of being transformed into His likeness will then be complete. Our lowly bodies will be transformed to be like His glorious body.

The heavenly host is moved to worship by the holiness of God and those nearest the throne fall before Him in homage and adoration. "Whenever the living creatures give glory, honour and thanks to him who sits on the throne and who lives for ever, the twenty-four elders fall down before him who sits on the throne, and worship him who lives for ever and ever." (Rev. 4:9–10)

If the holiness of God moves the heavenly creatures in such a way, and they are themselves holy, set apart for God, consecrated totally to His service, what must a revelation of God's holiness do to a mere man? Isaiah speaks for all who have encountered Him in such a way: "'Woe to me!' I cried. 'I am ruined! For I am a man of unclean lips, and I live among a people of unclean lips, and my eyes have seen the King, the Lord Almighty.'" (Is. 6:5)

Nobody can have even a glimpse of the holiness of God without being made aware immediately of his own unholiness before Him. There are no words that can describe the Lord in His majesty and holiness. All Isaiah, or anybody can do, is to speak of the consequences of such an experience. He felt totally and utterly unworthy, lost, ruined. He believed that no one could see the Lord and live; God was too great, mighty and holy for mortal man to behold and survive to tell of the experience. His immediate expectation must have been of death; "I am ruined!" I cannot survive this.

To him, it was as if the judgment had come and he was so aware, not only of his own impurity, but of the unholiness of the people: "I am a man of unclean lips and I live among a people of unclean lips."

One of the seraphs touches his lips with a live coal: "See, this has touched your lips: your guilt is taken away and your sin atoned for." (v. 7)

Isaiah is forgiven; he is made pure and holy in God's sight, and not through anything he has done himself. Now he can endure the presence of the Lord. More than that, he can have confidence and be bold before his God. So when the Lord's voice was heard asking, "Whom shall I send? And who will go for us?", Isaiah is quick in his response. "Here am I. Send me!"

One moment he feels he cannot endure the presence of the holy God; the next he is being commissioned to go to the people in His name. The cleansing that took place between those two moments was crucial.

ENCOUNTER WITH GOD

If God was to grant you such a revelation of Himself today, would your reaction be any different? You may have known the Lord Jesus for years as your Saviour and firmly believe all your sins to be forgiven, yet your cry for mercy would be greater, more intense, real, urgent, than at any previous time. Why? Because in the light of His Holiness you would see yourself more clearly than ever before. In the presence of the Sinless One you would grieve for your sins as never before. You would recognise the poverty of your love for God, the shallowness of your faith and how awful your disobedience.

You would see your heart more clearly and the selfish motives in your seeking of the Lord. You would understand how little you have really cared for Him and how much you have tried to use Him. You would be immediately aware of how you have loved sins which He has hated, how casual has been your approach to holiness. You would be aware of your failure to love others and of ungodly attitudes towards them. You would know the folly of standing in judgment on them when you are in such need of God's grace and mercy yourself.

You would have to face the futility of much of your thinking and activity. You would feel ashamed of how sterile your times of prayer had been, how half-hearted your seeking of the Lord, how you had neglected the living out of His Word.

And you would cry to the Lord. Yes, there would be tears and sorrow and grief and wailing before the Lord. Do not think your temperament would save you from that.

All these things would come pressing upon you one after another. You would be driven first to your knees and then on to your face before God.

At the same time you would be profoundly thankful for the atoning blood of Jesus. Tears of sorrow would give way to tears of joy. Because of that blood shed for your sins, you would know the merciful forgiveness of the Lord. From that moment you would value that blood more highly than ever before. You would know that it is only because of that sacrifice made for you, that you could experience the holiness of God and live.

Holy, holy, holy is the Lord God Almighty; the whole earth is full of his glory.

DRAW NEAR

Can we all expect to have such encounters with God as were given to Isaiah, Paul or John? Perhaps not; but it is the same God that we worship and He desires to reveal His holiness to all His children. We are told to fix our eyes on Jesus and draw near to God with confidence.

We need not fear to approach Him because we have the atoning blood of the Saviour already poured out for us. It is that blood that saves us from God's wrath and delivers us from the judgment we deserve. It is that blood that cleanses us from every sin the holiness of God lays bare. It is because of that blood we can have boldness to draw near to the throne of God's grace.

Without that blood, who would dare to meet with the living God? Every knee will one day have to bow to Jesus and every tongue make the confession that He is Lord. But what of those who have failed to acknowledge His authority during their earthly lives, who have used the name of Jesus as a curse or have not heeded His holy purposes? What of those who have not been cleansed by the blood of Jesus? They only have a "fearful expectation of judgment and of raging fire that will consume the enemies of God." (Heb. 10:27)

When you meet with the Lord in His holiness you will find yourself pleading for the lost. You will not tire of asking God to have mercy on sinners, even those that reach the very depths of depravity. You will be so aware of the cleansing power of Jesus' blood that you will know nothing is beyond God's forgiveness when people turn to Him in repentance. To God all men are depraved in their sinfulness and need to be washed in that blood. No one is beyond His reach or His salvation if only they will turn to Him.

If a man knows something of the holiness of God from personal experience, not a day will pass without him expressing his thankfulness for that redeeming sacrifice. He knows he stands in need daily of the forgiveness of God, not simply for sins committed, but for what he is in himself. For he will have caught a glimpse of what he really is as God sees him. One who is most definitely loved by God, but one who stands in need of His holiness. One who is accepted because of all that Jesus has done for him, but one who fails to live the holy and righteous life made possible by Him. "Therefore, brothers, since we have confidence to enter the Most Holy Place by the blood of Jesus, by a new and living way opened for us through the curtain, that is, his body, and since we have a great priest over the house of God, let us draw near to God with a sincere heart in full assurance of faith, having our hearts sprinkled to cleanse us from a guilty conscience and having our bodies washed with pure water." (Heb. 10:19–22)

WITH SINCERITY AND FAITH

Anyone who draws near to God in His holiness will need to approach Him with a "sincere heart in full assurance of faith". Sincerity of heart is essential for God is not going to reveal Himself readily to those who do not want to meet with Him. It is for you to draw near to Him and then He will draw near to you. And it takes time to seek the Lord. Your willingness to give Him that time is an indication of your sincerity and earnestness.

We need to approach the Lord in "full assurance of faith". He wants us to be perfectly assured that He does not draw us into His holy presence to devastate us, condemn us or reject us. He wants to reveal Himself to us and impress upon us the mark of His holiness, that it may be clearly seen we have been with Jesus. "Let us then approach the throne of grace with confidence, so that we may receive mercy and find grace to help us in our time of need." (Heb. 4:16)

To fix our eyes on Jesus is not only to look at His example in the days of His humanity, but to see Him as He is now reigning as the King of Righteousness. He is the High Priest who has offered Himself to the Father in order that we might be raised to the throne of heaven; "such a high priest meets our need – one who is holy, blameless, pure, set apart from sinners, exalted above the heavens." (Heb. 7:26) That sinless offering had to be made only once, and all who identify with that work on the Cross are made acceptable to God. The blood which He shed keeps us guiltless before the Lord as we allow Him to cleanse us afresh in it. "How much more, then, will the blood of Christ, who through the eternal Spirit offered himself unblemished to God, cleanse our consciences from acts that lead to death, so that we may serve the living God." (Heb. 9:14)

The man who has a heart for the purposes of God is not concerned about personal holiness as an end in itself; he wants to serve the living God. His effectiveness in service and ministry will depend on his personal encounter with Him.

The consequences of such encounters will lead to the heart-rending realisation of his nothingness. The fruit of those experiences will be an increased desire to have done with sin, greater determination to walk in obedience to Him and, above all, an increased awareness of who He is and, therefore, a greater love for Him. The holy presence of the

Lord will go with him from the place of prayer and then will come the learning process as to how it is possible to stay in that holy place with God, how to walk on the highway of holiness.

Does this deter you from seeking the Lord? Does this put you off from meeting with God in His holiness? Do you think it would be better to remain as you are without encountering Him in such a way?

One day you will have to meet Him face to face. Will it be too late then? Is it not better to be cleansed by the blood of Jesus now, for God to reveal all that is ungodly about your heart and life in order that you might repent and walk in newness of life, radiating more of the holiness of your God? Better the refining fire now, than the fire of judgment later! And what a mighty privilege to be drawn into the holy presence of God most high!

Let us draw near to God with a sincere heart in full assurance of faith.

14. MADE HOLY

God wants to refine you, perfect you, make you holy like Jesus. That is the work He undertakes in the life of every Christian. It is called "being sanctified".

Don't let long words like "sanctification" deter you. Sanctification is the process by which God will continue to work in your life to make you more and more like Himself. There are two distinct meanings of this word sanctification and great confusion can result if they are not distinguished.

CONSECRATION

First, sanctification involves consecration. Remember that the basic meaning of "holy" is "set apart". The person who is "holy" is the one who is "set apart for God". He is set apart FOR God because he has been set apart BY God. He has exercised his free will to respond to God's call, for his conversion is essentially a response to God's initiative. He is yielding himself to the Lord and recognising His ownership of his life. He is consecrating himself to the Lord, to be a "set apart" child of God, called to live for the glory of God.

Consecration comes before and after justification. We give ourselves to the Lord in response to His love, are born again and justified, fully accepted in God's sight as the blood of Jesus cleanses us from all the sin of our former life. He declares that we are righteous in His sight. "But you were washed, you were sanctified, you were justified in the name of the Lord Jesus Christ and by the Spirit of our God." (1 Cor. 6:11)

Often the Gospel is offered to people as the way to be

blessed and to receive all they want from God. It is indeed the way of blessing and there is no more joyful life than living with Jesus. But our desires need to be consecrated to His desires, so that we want what He wants. HAPPINESS DOES NOT PRODUCE HOLINESS, BUT HOLINESS BRINGS HAPPINESS, the joy of knowing that God is working His purpose out in us.

We misunderstand the Gospel if we imagine God wants to share our unholy lives with us and bend His will to ours, pouring out His abundance so that all our fleshly whims and fancies are provided. He calls us to deny our self-lives, take up our cross daily and follow Him.

A man is not pronounced righteous and acceptable to God (justified) unless he is consecrated or set apart for God (sanctified). If he is not willing to yield himself wholeheartedly to God he is not justified, will have no assurance of the forgiveness of his sins or that God has accepted him, and he will not manifest a transformed life.

He may claim to be a Christian, know much about the Bible and Christian doctrine and involve himself in the life and politics of a church. But that lack of consecration prevents him experiencing the new birth without which a man cannot enter the Kingdom of God. So a man is not justified (made righteous and acceptable to God) unless he is sanctified (consecrated to Him).

At the same time God undertakes the sanctification of the man who is justified. And here we come to the second meaning of "sanctification".

PROGRESSIVE IMPROVEMENT

Having accepted the new believer and having declared him righteous, the Lord calls him to live in righteousness, to do what is right in His sight, to be obedient to the leading of the Holy Spirit at all times.

God is well aware that the new believer will fail to be completely obedient because of his desire to sin. He will need to consecrate himself to the service of his Lord again and again, and ask for His forgiveness whenever he sins.

The Lord knows of the unholiness that persists in the believer's life.

God sees you in Jesus. He sees you already made righteous, acceptable, holy even. He sees you already reigning in glory. That is the position Jesus has given you because of all He has done for you, a position that no man could attain for himself.

And yet you will only reflect that position in a very imperfect way. So God undertakes your sanctification – to make you holy, to make you like Jesus, changing you from one degree of glory to another. This is a progressive work that God Himself undertakes, and He will bring it to completion. He sees it already accomplished, but has to take you through the various stages in your experience to enable its fulfilment.

This may seem like a strange paradox. You are made holy and yet called to be holy. "We have been made holy through the sacrifice of the body of Jesus Christ once for all;" (Heb. 10:10), and yet "by one sacrifice he has made perfect for ever those who are being made holy." (Heb. 10:14)

So God sees you already sanctified in Jesus, in both senses of that word. He sees you consecrated to Himself and made holy and perfect in His sight. And yet He teaches you that you need to be continually consecrated, given totally to Him and set apart for Him. He needs to continue the work of bringing about changes in your character that will make you more like Jesus and increase your holiness.

A small child will appear very different by the time he is an adult. As he matures he will change in many ways, but he will be the same person with the same identity. Sanctification is something like this.

God knows you, not only as you are now, but as you will be. He sees you as an immature child when you first come to know Him, but also as the mature adult believer you will become. He even sees you already perfected, reigning in glory with Jesus.

At the same time He undertakes to lead you through the

various stages of growth so that you will become like Him, changed from one degree of glory to another. His Spirit lives in you to bring about those changes and yet you will remain the same person, with the same identity.

You can take comfort that God never fails to do what He sets out to do. If He says that He will make you like Jesus so that when you see Him you shall be like Him, then He will do just that. What He requires from you is cooperation in His purpose.

Justification (making him acceptable to God) is the work of God FOR the Christian. Sanctification (making him like God) is the work of God IN the believer. Both are His work and therefore are the product of His grace, of the love that He has for us and that we do not deserve. No man can justify himself, neither can he sanctify himself. By yielding himself to the Lord he is already justified and is being sanctified by the work of the Holy Spirit in his life.

That is the truth about you. So rejoice in the Lord!

We have been made holy through the sacrifice of the body of Jesus Christ once for all.

To speak of the progressive work of sanctification in no way undermines our faith in the position we have before God. To know that you are made holy in Jesus will be a great encouragement to you in living out your daily life in holiness.

If you start the day knowing that you are accepted by God, forgiven, made righteous and holy in His sight because of Jesus, you can have confidence to know that by trusting the power of the Holy Spirit, it is possible for you to live in holiness throughout that day.

If, however, you doubt what Jesus has done for you and believe yourself to be unacceptable, unrighteous and unholy, you have condemned yourself. The most you can achieve is to strive with all your might to think, speak and act like Jesus, knowing that you are bound to fail.

To say that you are righteous and holy in God's sight does

not mean that you claim to have reached a state of instant perfection. It is simply to state the truth to which the Scriptures testify.

How can we say we are righteous when it is obvious that not everything about us is right? How can we say that we are holy even though we know that in many ways we are not like Jesus in character, and our consecration to Him often appears half-hearted?

IN CHRIST

We are righteous and holy only because we are "in Christ Jesus", because we live in God. That is where He put us when we first turned to Him in true repentance: "It is because of him that you are in Christ Jesus, who has become for us wisdom from God – that is, our righteousness, holiness and redemption." (1 Cor. 1:30)

God has taken hold of your life and put you into Christ that you might live out your life in Him. Jesus told His disciples: "Remain in me, and I will remain in you." (John 15:4) Nobody can remain where he has not been put! You have been put into Jesus, so stay in Him: that is the word of Jesus to all disciples.

If you take a piece of paper and place it in a book it will go wherever the book is taken, as long as it remains in the book. If it falls out, it is on its own again. When Jesus tells us to abide in Him it is as if He tells us to be like that piece of paper, submitted to Him and willing to go wherever He goes. When we rebel and choose to be deliberately disobedient we slip out of His will.

God loves you so much He has chosen to put you in His Son and His purpose is for you to live in Him. And what does He promise as a result? "If a man remains in me and I in him, he will bear much fruit; apart from me you can do nothing." (v. 5)

Those are the alternatives for any Christian: to remain in Jesus and be fruitful or strive in his own strength and live in his own way accomplishing nothing. Jesus goes on to warn:

"If anyone does not remain in me, he is like a branch that is thrown away and withers; such branches are picked up, thrown into the fire and burned." (v. 6)

This is a solemn warning and presents the Christian with a clear ultimatum. There can be only one right way: remain in Jesus, abide in Him, go on continuously living in Him. (The Greek word is in a continuous tense.)

ABIDE IN LOVE

What does it mean in practice to remain in Jesus? He anticipates the question by telling the disciples to "remain in my love."

He is love. To live in Him is to live in love. To walk in His ways is to walk in the ways of love, expressing His love in thought, attitude, word and action. To walk in love is to walk in obedience to Jesus. "If you obey my commands, you will remain in my love, just as I have obeyed my Father's commands and remain in his love." (v. 10)

It was imperative in the days of His humanity for Jesus to remain in His Father's love and that was only possible because He was prepared to obey His Father in everything. If that was true for Jesus, it must be as true for His disciples. And all believers are called to live as disciples of the risen Lord. To live in obedience to Jesus will result in living in love. He will not ask anything of us that is unloving, although we will discover that His concept of love differs considerably from the soft, sentimental idea of love that some people attribute to Him.

St John, who records these words of Jesus and was present when they were spoken, wrote his First Epistle some fifty years after the Last Supper. They were fifty years of reflection upon these truths but, above all, fifty years of experiencing them. He writes: "This is how we know we are in him: Whoever claims to live in him must walk as Jesus did." (1 John 2:5–6)

John goes on to say that the anointing we receive from God teaches us to remain in Him. The Holy Spirit within us urges us to remain in Jesus, to walk as He did and to be like Him. God does not leave it to our own initiative, to try and live in Jesus by our own efforts. It was His act to put us into His Son and it is only by trusting to the leading of His Spirit that we will effectively remain in Him.

Christians want to be fruitful in the ministries to which God has called them. Many do not realise that the more like Jesus they are in character, the more effective they will be in ministry.

God does not ask us to consecrate ourselves to some act of service or particular ministry – but to Him! "In him is no sin. No one who lives in him keeps on sinning. No one who continues to sin has either seen him or known him." (1 John 3:5–6)

NOT IN SIN

The argument is simple. In the Holy God there could be no sin. To live in Him involves turning away from a life of sin. To continue to sin would be a denial of our position in Jesus. The man who is content to remain in sinful ways has no real knowledge or experience of God.

John is not advocating perfectionist thinking. He is speaking of wilfully, deliberately and knowingly continuing to sin. The one who deliberately sins cannot have much love for Jesus. But John does not say that he will never ever commit another sin. If he loves Jesus, he will want to obey Him, not grieve Him by wilful disobedience. The one who lives in Jesus cannot live in sin; he will not habitually displease his Lord. "He who does what is right is righteous, just as he is righteous." (v. 7)

Is there some way in which you are grieving the Lord because of deliberate disobedience or indiscipline? Has God been asking something of you and met with stubborn refusal on your part? Is there some area of sin which is totally inconsistent with living in Jesus? If so, come to Him with repentance now and let Him deal with you. The one who lives in Jesus does not continue to sin.

*If a man remains in me and I in him, he will bear much fruit;
apart from me you can do nothing.*

POSITION AND PERFORMANCE

Some believe it is possible to reach a state of perfection
instantaneously by an act of faith. Such perfection, in which
a man does not knowingly or willingly sin again, is not for
this life. We know our position before God as those who are
made holy in Jesus. That truth comes to our hearts through
faith. But we recognise, at the same time, our failure to live
that life to perfection. Only Jesus has accomplished that.

Jesus is the Author of our faith. It would be wonderful if
He gave us such a gift of faith that we never sinned again.
Even Paul did not claim to have reached such spiritual
heights. Instead he says, "By faith we eagerly await
through the Spirit the righteousness for which we hope."
(Gal. 5:5) He does not doubt for a minute the state of
righteousness before God that is his in Christ. But he is
acknowledging that the performance does not match the
position. He knows well the pull of temptation and the
danger of preaching one thing and doing another, of having
the right doctrine without the right life. And so he says: "I
beat my body and make it my slave so that after I have
preached to others, I myself will not be disqualified for the
prize." (1 Cor. 9:27)

Towards the end of his life, Paul wrote the Letter to the
Philippians, which contains many great faith-building statements. He also gives a sober estimate of his own life and
attitudes: sober, but not lacking in faith. "I consider everything a loss compared to the surpassing greatness of knowing Christ Jesus my Lord, for whose sake I have lost all
things. I consider them rubbish, that I may gain Christ and
be found in him, not having any righteousness of my own
that comes from the law, but that which is through faith in
Christ – the righteousness that comes from God and is by
faith." (Phil. 3:8–9)

That is his position before God; made righteous by his

faith in what Christ has done for him. He continues: "I want to know Christ and the power of his resurrection and the fellowship of sharing in his sufferings, becoming like him in death, and so, somehow to attain to the resurrection from the dead." (vv. 10–11)

Is Paul lacking in faith or assurance? Not at all! A man who is convinced that he is made righteous through Christ must know Him personally and be in a living relationship with Him. And yet Paul says here that he wants to know Christ. He is talking of the progressive work of His Spirit making him more like Jesus. Although he has experienced the Saviour in many ways, he sees the need to be like Him in "sharing in his sufferings, becoming like him in death". Notice that he uses the word "becoming".

Paul is well aware of the frailty of human flesh and knows that he needs to prove faithful to the end, even to the point of death. And his hope is the certain hope of all believers: that he may attain to the resurrection from the dead. "Not that I have already obtained all this, or have already been made perfect, but I press on to take hold of that for which Christ Jesus took hold of me. Brothers, I do not consider myself yet to have taken hold of it. But one thing I do: Forgetting what is behind and straining towards what is ahead, I press on towards the goal to win the prize for which God has called me heavenward in Christ Jesus." (vv. 12 –14)

Christ took hold of Paul's life to make him holy. He has the same purpose for your life. Paul wants to take hold of the perfection for which Christ took hold of him. He does not want to miss God's ultimate purpose; he is ready to cooperate with Him.

LOOKING FORWARD

How can he do this? Not by constantly looking back. Not by constantly regretting the past, excusing his failure, imagining his real faults are due to past experiences or traumas.

He will move on in God's purposes of holiness and perfection only by looking to what lies ahead.

Holiness is not achieved by looking at yourself but at Jesus. You can look in upon yourself and soon be rendered spiritually paralysed, conscious of your sinfulness, failure and unworthiness.

Or you can look forward, knowing that it is not what you have been that matters, but what God is making you, what you are becoming in Jesus. That will increase your determination to remain faithful to the One who alone has the power to forgive sin and make you like Himself. You will rejoice in Him at all times, as Paul learned to do, knowing that every situation in your life is being used by God for your good to bring you to the fulfilment of His purpose for you, when you will receive the crown of life.

"All of us who are mature should take such a view of things. And if on some point you think differently, that too God will make clear to you. Only let us live up to what we have already attained." (vv. 15–16) Paul sees the work of salvation as completed in Christ and yet being worked out in his life. It embraces the progressive work of sanctification as well as the finished work of justification.

The man who cares little for holiness cares little for what God holds most precious. The Christian who is willing to cooperate with the Lord can have every confidence that He will complete what He has begun.

FAITH AND HUMILITY

The man of faith will not be a man of presumption. If he knows the holiness of his God, he will never forget his own unholiness apart from Him. He will not be looking at himself with morbid introspection. But he will know what it is to bow low before the throne of God in true humility knowing that, of himself, he is and always will be, totally unworthy of God's love and acceptance. And yet, at the same time, he will rejoice in the blood that cleanses and through which he is made acceptable. He will be thankful for the grace and mercy of the Lord who has called and chosen him to be a child of God and who has destined him for the courts of heaven. He will tread carefully through life not wanting to offend the Lord who has shown him such love, never presuming an inheritance he could not deserve.

And yet he will walk confidently through life, coming with boldness before the throne of God because he knows he is accepted and counted righteous. What a paradox! But how precious to see in a believer the confidence of the one who knows he is accepted and the humility of the one who knows he is nothing before the great Almighty God.

It is more common to find Christians who manifest one or the other. Either they radiate a faith that seems to border at times on pride and reflects little humility or brokenness. They are forever speaking of their exploits of faith as if they are somehow responsible (at least in part) for the mighty things God has done. Or you find believers who have such a sense of nothingness and total unworthiness that they dare not believe God would do anything of significance for them. How blest is the one in whom these two virtues of faith and humility come together and live in harmony.

The Lord wants to see both coming together in your life. Remember that holiness is not only being emptied of self; it is being full of the life of Jesus and that involves being full of faith, expecting God to do mighty things in your experience and through you in the lives of others. It is not only being emptied of the negative, but also being filled with the positive. The refining fire purges you of the impurities that your life may be filled with the fire of His love.

"Join with others in following my example, brothers." (Phil. 3:17) Paul is often accused of pride because he dares to make such statements. What lack of insight there is in such an accusation! It is only a man broken of self-pleasing and humble before his God who would dare to make such a statement. How many preachers have you heard daring to say: "Follow my example, believers, of living the life of Jesus"?

Most would not dare, because they know only too well

the poverty of their own hearts before God. They may speak of their exploits of faith and suggest you follow their example in believing God to work miraculously. Such testimony has its place. But it is only the one who has been stripped of pride who would dare to say: "Look at my example."

Others look to you for example; they rightly expect to see something of Jesus in you, His love and willingness to serve. Jesus is wanting you to follow His example of faith working through love. Then they will see you persevering in faith even through adverse circumstances, able to believe God to intervene with His almighty power to change circumstances. And you will be more effective in ministering to others in their need with the faith and love that come from the Holy Spirit.

Forgetting what is behind and straining towards what is ahead, I press on towards the goal to win the prize for which God has called me heavenward in Christ Jesus.

15.   KINGDOM INHERITANCE

The Sermon on the Mount is teaching about practical holiness and begins with the Beatitudes. Jesus promises the faithful that they shall possess the Kingdom of Heaven, will inherit the whole earth, will be comforted and filled by God; they will be shown mercy, will see God and will be known as the sons of God. No wonder Jesus describes such people as "blessed", which the Amplified Bible defines as: "happy, to be envied, and spiritually prosperous (that is, with life, joy and satisfaction in God's favour and salvation, regardless of their outward conditions)". (Matt. 5:3) How does Jesus describe those who will receive such a rich inheritance?

First He says that the poor in spirit are blessed "for theirs is the kingdom of heaven". (Matt. 5:3) The poor in spirit are those who are humble before the Lord. They recognise their own unworthiness and need of Him, not because of their personal negative feelings, but because God is who He is.

Even the greatest of saints knows his nothingness before God. He may realise he is loved, forgiven, accepted, justified, redeemed, filled with the Spirit, a son of God, living in Christ Jesus; but he will never lose sight of his nothingness. Of himself he could never deserve any of this rich inheritance God has chosen to give him by His grace and mercy. He will not presume upon God but will walk humbly before Him and before men, not wanting to miss the Lord's best purposes for his life.

THE HUMBLE MAN

The humble man knows well that if he slips into pride, he will miss God's best until he is humbled once again. He will be determined to walk closely with Jesus and will not be afraid of rebuke or correction, for he has submitted all to the sovereignty of Jesus. He wants Him to exercise His authority over every part of his life. The Kingdom of heaven is his by God's direct gift and he will want his life to be a worthy reflection of the life of that Kingdom. Then the life of that Kingdom can be communicated to others and he will be part of the answer to the prayer given by Jesus that God's Kingdom may come and His will be done on earth as in heaven.

The humble man will be overawed by the generosity of his God, by the profusion of spiritual and material riches that are poured into his life, for he will taste the abundant wealth of that Kingdom life. To have his needs satisfied would be enough, but he discovers that his Lord gives far more than the minimum required to supply his needs; He gives abundantly. When the Lord leaves him in want for a time it is always for a purpose, part of the refining and building of faith that God lovingly works out in him.

So the man who is poor in spirit is a contented man, no matter what his circumstances. Like Paul he will say, "I have learned to be content whatever the circumstances. I know what it is to be in need, and I know what it is to have plenty. I have learned the secret of being content in any and every situation, whether well fed or hungry, whether living in plenty or in want. I can do everything through him who gives me strength." (Phil. 4:11–13)

That kind of man knows what it is to be "joyful always; pray continually; give thanks in all circumstances, for this is God's will for you in Christ Jesus." (1 Thess. 5:16–18) He will have been submitted to the Lord's will and be a man of resolute faith; not perhaps the brash faith that is sometimes manifested by the spiritually immature, but the steadfast faith that recognises that every detail of his life is in the

Lord's hands and that He will never leave him, fail him or forsake him.

His total reliance is on the Lord: "apart from me you can do nothing." (John 15:5) He not only quotes those words, he believes them; so much so that he attempts to trust Jesus in every situation. Failure to do so will mean he will inevitably sink back into self-effort. He recognises his need of God in every situation.

The poor in spirit do not restrict their worship of God to Sundays or their prayer to a minimum; neither do they neglect their study of His Word. To live Kingdom life they know their dependence on the King of heaven, their need to hear and obey what He says. They recognise their weakness and vulnerability and therefore they praise and exalt the King. They do not draw attention to themselves but to Him. They want everyone to know Him, that He is the Lord of grace and mercy who "chose the foolish things of the world to shame the wise; God chose the weak things of this world to shame the strong. He chose the lowly things of this world and the despised things – and the things that are not – to nullify the things that are, so that no one may boast before him." (1 Cor. 1:27–29)

The humble man discovers that the more he is submitted to the authority of the King, the more His kingly authority can be seen in his life. He does not need to resort to authoritarianism or try to impress others with extravagant claims as to his spirituality or effectiveness. He knows his status before God and the resources of His Kingdom made available to him. He never ceases to be amazed at the grace of his God and he knows that he doesn't deserve to be a servant, and yet God has made him a son.

You are one of God's blessed ones for He has called and chosen you to be His holy child, to have the inheritance of His Kingdom, and therefore to walk humbly before men and before God. You have recognised your need of Him or you would not be a Christian. How is the reflection of Jesus in your life hindered through pride? Do you grumble and complain about your circumstances, or do you recognise

His sovereignty over all the details of your life? Do you still try to solve your own problems and work things out for yourself, or do you know that apart from Him you can do nothing? If so, you are content to trust Him with resolute, unyielding faith in the Lord who has called you to such a rich inheritance.

Blessed are the poor in spirit, for theirs is the kingdom of heaven.

COMFORT

Jesus says: "Blessed are those who mourn, for they shall be comforted." (Matt. 5:4) The humble man will know what it is to mourn. He will grieve when he offends the Lord, yields to temptation or falls into any act of sin or disobedience. There will be times when he will weep before the Lord because he knows his own unworthiness while recognising the abundant goodness of the Lord to him.

However his eyes will not remain on himself. Like Isaiah he knows something of the holiness of his God and so his cry will be: "I am a man of unclean lips, and I live among a people of unclean lips, and my eyes have seen the King, the Lord Almighty." (Is. 6:5) He will grieve and weep before the Lord, not only for himself, but for the sins of the Church and the world. He longs to see the holiness and righteousness of God not only reflected more fully in his own life, but in all God's children and in the society in which he lives.

That does not mean that he will look upon others with self-righteous pride or scornful judgment. No, his prayer is not: "Forgive them, O Lord," but "Forgive us." He identifies with those for whom he intercedes. He rejoices with those who rejoice, and weeps with those who weep. He feels the lostness, the emptiness, the hopelessness of those who do not know Jesus, and he mourns for them and prays for them and rejoices over every spiritual captive that is delivered from bondage.

The humble man who mourns will know what it is to be

comforted by his Lord, to have the "everlasting arms" about him. In Scripture to comfort is to strengthen, not merely to sympathise or console. He shares God's grief and sorrow over the lost and destitute, but never loses sight of the Lord's victory on Calvary where every human need and dilemma was met. He will be comforted from what he knows of the faithfulness of God, His love, compassion, gentleness, patience and mercy. He will daily be comforted and strengthened by the Word of God and in prayer. He will never be far away from the personal touch of God on his life to strengthen and sustain him, to encourage and give him vision.

To be "poor in spirit" is not a negative attribute, but the positive virtue of humility in a Christian's life that releases God's activity through him into the lives of other people. Similarly, there is no need to apologise for those who "mourn". If only there were more born again, Spirit-filled, Kingdom-conscious Christians who knew what it was to mourn before God and know, not only that He is victorious, but that they have the anointing from heaven to bring that victory through intercessory prayer into hopeless lives.

Again we see Paul as an example of what Jesus taught: "I speak the truth in Christ – I am not lying, my conscience confirms it in the Holy Spirit – I have great sorrow and unceasing anguish in my heart. For I could wish that I myself were cursed and cut off from Christ for the sake of my brothers." (Rom. 9:1–3)

The man who mourns is ready to do more than pray for those who are lost, he will be prepared to suffer considerable hardships for the sake of the Gospel. Paul was no stranger to this: "Rather, as servants of God we commend ourselves in every way: in great endurance; in troubles, hardships and distresses; in beatings, imprisonments and riots; in hard work, sleepless nights and hunger; in purity, understanding, patience and kindness; in the Holy Spirit and in sincere love; in truthful speech and in the power of God; with weapons of righteousness in the right hand and in the left; through glory and dishonour, bad report and good report; genuine, yet regarded as imposters; known, yet regarded as unknown; dying, and yet we live on; beaten, and yet not killed; sorrowful, yet always rejoicing; poor, yet making many rich; having nothing, and yet possessing everything." (2 Cor. 6:4–10)

We can only try to imagine the grief and sorrow that Paul experienced. Yet his testimony makes it clear that he did not lose heart or see himself as defeated. Rather, he rejoiced always and was confident that God used every personal setback for the good of His Kingdom. A man could not endure such hardship with these positive attitudes unless he was "comforted" by the presence of the Lord, knowing His empowering strength. He could not have persevered through such difficulties unless he was sure of his heavenly reward.

Do you ever heed James' words to "grieve, mourn and wail", to humble yourself before the Lord? (James 4:9–10) Do you know what it is to grieve not only for your own sins but for the sins of others – not only their problems and difficult circumstances? Have you wept before the Lord for the sins of His Church generally, or the particular fellowship to which you belong? Do you plead with God for the unconverted, especially your loved ones, your close friends and relatives? Do you identify with those for whom you pray, knowing their lostness without Jesus?

If you do, you know the comfort of the Lord. You taste the depths of His mercy and kindness, and understand that He resolves situations when you become truly serious about them and are willing to give yourself to Him in prayer on behalf of others.

Blessed are those who mourn, for they shall be comforted.

MEEKNESS

Jesus said: "Blessed are the meek, for they will inherit the earth." (Matt. 5:5) Jesus sees meekness as a positive virtue, not a weak failure. To be weak before God is often to be bold before men.

The love of God is such that He does not hit back when we hurt or grieve Him, when we disobey or neglect Him. On the Cross Jesus absorbed all the bitterness and hatred that was directed at Him and merely forgave those responsible for His crucifixion: "Father, forgive them, for they do not know what they are doing." (Luke 23:34)

He taught the people their need to forgive instead of holding on to hurt or seeking revenge. "For if you forgive men when they sin against you, your heavenly Father will also forgive you. But if you do not forgive men their sins, your Father will not forgive your sins." (Matt. 6:14–15)

It is more difficult to forgive than to inwardly fume with indignation and hurt. God expects His children to forgive for, as His holy ones, He calls them to reflect His own attitudes and actions. So Jesus tells us to "turn the other cheek", to love our enemies and pray for those who abuse us.

It requires meekness to trust the Lord to vindicate you when you are wronged, to avoid the temptation to justify yourself before others. That is what He desires, that you entrust your cause to the Lord and leave it with Him. It is one of the Christian virtues that can only be expressed in the midst of difficult circumstances. Like Jesus we learn to love by absorbing all the negative things that are directed at us and say or do nothing in return, except forgive and pray.

The Lord loves meekness, for it is His way. It is the meek who will inherit the earth; it is they who will exert powerful influence for the work of the Gospel in the world. In the end, the victory goes to those who react as Jesus did.

The flesh fights hard against any virtue that the Spirit of God wants to develop in us. That is certainly true of meekness. The self-life screams against such humble reactions to opposition. But the man who truly desires to be like Jesus has to yield his reputation to the Lord. It matters little how others speak of him or malign him, God knows the truth and He will vindicate those who faithfully obey Him and deal with those who oppose them. Jesus made Himself "of no reputation" when He humbled Himself and came among us as our Saviour.

A love of reputation is one of the gravest spiritual diseases within the Church, not least among some ministers of the Gospel. To hold on to reputation is to deny meekness. While a man contends for his own reputation, he fights for himself. Where would Paul or the other apostles have been if they were concerned to guard their reputations? How the cause of the Gospel would have been hindered! "We are fools for Christ, but you are so wise in Christ! We are weak, but you are strong! You are honoured, we are dishonoured! . . . When we are cursed, we bless; when we are persecuted, we endure it; when we are slandered, we answer kindly." (1 Cor. 4:10,12–13)

There is a quiet courage that is needed to manifest meekness in this way. The motive is to glorify Jesus, to react as He would so that His life might be demonstrated and communicated to others.

Does your reputation still matter to you? Do you fight hard to defend yourself? Are you concerned how others think of you? Perhaps you fear men more than you fear God, spending considerable nervous energy trying to hide from others what you know is clear to Him. Will you allow your reputation to go to the Cross? You will be more effective in your witness in the world if you do, for it is the meek who will inherit the earth.

What suffers when our reputation suffers? Only pride – and we long for God to break us of every vestige of that.

Blessed are the meek, for they will inherit the earth.

RIGHTEOUSNESS

Jesus said: "Blessed are those who hunger and thirst for righteousness, for they will be filled." (Matt. 5:6) Such hunger begins in the heart. It is a deep inner desire to live a life of righteousness, because that is the only kind of life that is pleasing to God.

The convicted sinner longs to be forgiven, to be rid of his sense of guilt, to know that he is cleansed and approved of by God. To know that he is made righteous through the blood of Jesus is a wonderful revelation to him. But the Christian who wishes to glorify God in his life does not leave matters there. He will not be content unless that righteous state is expressed in righteous action, holy thinking and godly attitudes. So he is hungry and thirsty for the work of God's Spirit in his life to be such that he obeys the Lord and walks in His ways.

Jesus promises that the one who is hungry to reflect the presence of God in his life will be filled to overflowing with His Spirit of holiness, righteousness, love, joy, peace and power. In other words, he will be full of Jesus.

To be filled with the Spirit is not a single experience in a Christian's life. When his hunger and thirst for the Lord's righteous ways diminishes then it seems that the life and vitality of the Spirit's work within him also diminishes. It is not that God's Spirit has lost any of His power, but simply that the Christian is no longer living immersed in that power of love. He has lost his motivation to do so.

If the intensity of the Spirit's activity diminishes, then faith too diminishes and he will soon be back to a life of striving to please God by his own efforts, or mechanically going through the routine of prayer, worship and witness, knowing that he lacks the essential vitality that once he had. Small wonder that his effectiveness and fruitfulness seem also to diminish at such a time, for Jesus cannot be seen in self-effort and disobedience.

His protestations that he has been filled with the Spirit, is filled and always will be filled, helps him little in his dilemma. He may cry to God for fresh experience, another anointing, a further blessing. Ultimately he will have to face the issue about himself first: he has lost his hunger and thirst for God's righteousness in his life.

When he realises this and comes back humbly to the

Cross, he finds the Lord waiting for him with patience, love and forgiveness. As the priorities in his life are restored to their right order, so he experiences a fresh release of God's Spirit surging powerfully through his life. Faith is not only restored but deepened; the love of God melts the coldness that had been enveloping his heart; and, once again, the joy of praying is restored and answers begin to flow. He is aware again of the Lord's flow of provision and His care about all the practical details of his daily experience. Once again he is filled full of Jesus.

God wants consistency in our lives: to live in His fullness and to know His fullness in us. When we hunger only for blessings we miss what He intends. When we thirst for His righteousness and His ways, for His praise, honour and glory, then we know His fullness.

Paul tells the Ephesians that it is by being rooted and grounded in love that they will have the power to know the extent of His love, "That you may be filled to the measure of all the fullness of God." (Eph. 3:19) To the Colossians he says: "For in Christ all the fullness of the Deity lives in bodily form, and you have been given fullness in Christ." (Col. 2:9–10) That is what Jesus Himself promised: "I have come that they may have life, and have it to the full." (John 10:10)

God wants you to live in that fullness, never being content unless the power of the Holy Spirit is flowing out from our innermost being as rivers of living water, so that others around you receive Jesus through you. The test is always to see how much love is flowing towards God in your devotion to Him and towards others in practical ways.

Do you hunger and thirst to live in right ways with God? Are you concerned to see the areas of sin and disobedience in your life dealt with so that you can be full of the Spirit of Jesus? Has the love of God grown cold in your heart; are you returning to a life of striving, or has prayer become lifeless and mechanical? If so, Jesus is waiting to receive you with patience, love and forgiveness, to cleanse you of

all unrighteousness and enable you to live in His fullness of
life.

*Blessed are those who hunger and thirst for righteousness,
for they will be filled.*

MERCY

One of the spiritual principles that Jesus teaches is: "Give,
and it will be given to you." (Luke 6:38) This principle
is applicable to several different aspects of His teaching, including mercy. The man of God knows his need of
mercy, and that he is to be merciful to others. "Blessed
are the merciful; for they will be shown mercy." (Matt.
5:7)

The parable of the unmerciful servant is a warning to us
all. The master forgave the servant's great debt, but the
servant refused to forgive the paltry amount owed him by a
fellow servant. "You wicked servant" was the judgment of
the master. "Shouldn't you have had mercy on your fellow
servant just as I had on you?" (Matt. 18:33)

To show mercy to others is to reflect something of the
essential nature of God in His dealings with men. If He
were to deal with us as we deserve, He would wipe us from
the face of the earth and have nothing more to do with us.
Instead, in His love, He has shown His mercy in giving His
Son to be our Saviour, that, through Him we might obtain
mercy. "Because of his great love for us, God, who is rich in
mercy, made us alive with Christ." (Eph. 2:5)

Having tasted the mercy of God, what response does He
look for in His children? "Therefore, I urge you, brothers,
IN VIEW OF GOD'S MERCY, to offer your bodies as living
sacrifices, holy and pleasing to God – which is your spiritual worship." (Rom. 12:1) We are to give ourselves
wholeheartedly to the Lord to be holy and pleasing to Him.
This is the true spiritual worship He desires.

The world shows little mercy. In showing mercy to others

the Christian is demonstrating how totally different God's ways are from the ways of man.

The godly man will show meekness when opposed or reviled; he will also show mercy to those who wrong him, even when they are proved wrong, for love "keeps no record of wrongs". (1 Cor. 13:5) If he has tasted the mercy of God himself, his desire is that others too should know that mercy. If that mercy can be experienced, even imperfectly, through his loving responses to others that is to the good. For it is when people see Jesus in others that they are often urged to seek Him for themselves.

The man who shows mercy will often feel he is taken advantage of, that his opponents use his loving response for their own ends. They may even intensify their opposition; but he knows it is right to continue to show love, mercy and forgiveness. "Lord, how many times shall I forgive my brother?" Peter asked Jesus. He suggested seven as being the optimum number. "I tell you, not seven times, but seventy times seven," Jesus replied. That is mercy.

Those who show such mercy will never cease to be amazed at the love and goodness of the Lord in His patience with them as He slowly refines them and removes from them the impurities that mar His image in them.

BE MERCIFUL

Is there anyone from whom you are withholding mercy and forgiveness? Have you allowed bitterness or resentment to creep into your heart because you feel wronged by someone? Perhaps you have been holding on to a hurt for years and the Holy Spirit gently brings this matter before you now. It could be something from childhood or an event that occurred today.

As you show mercy and forgiveness you will be increasingly aware of God's mercy towards you. It pleases Him that you reflect His image. That bitterness within you is replaced with love and thankfulness.

Holding on to hurts not only offends God but causes you

untold harm. There are many who do not receive healing they need from God until first they are prepared to have mercy on others. The withholding of forgiveness can even cause physical, as well as emotional, distress and pain.

LOVING POSITIVELY

Mercy needs to be expressed not only in forgiveness, but in reaching out with love to meet the needs of others. In His mercy God has reached out to you with the life of Jesus. Has He been asking you to give to someone and you have been refusing, either through fear or because you have not wanted to do what He has asked? "If anyone has material possessions and sees his brother in need but has no pity on him, how can the love of God be in him?" (1 John 3:17)

Jesus teaches us not only to forgive our enemies but to pray for them and to bless those who act spitefully towards us. To Him mercy is doing something positive, not only resisting the negative. At the end of the parable of the Good Samaritan, when Jesus asks who acted as neighbour to the man who had been beaten and robbed, the legal expert replied: "The one who had mercy on him." To which Jesus said, "Go and do likewise."

"With the measure you use, it will be measured to you." (Matt. 7:2) Is He asking you to have mercy on someone in particular, by giving to him or loving him in some particular way? When you respond you will know the joy of pleasing your Lord and you can be sure that His mercy is extended to you.

Blessed are the merciful; for they will be shown mercy.

A PURE HEART

Jesus said: "Blessed are the pure in heart, for they will see God." (Matt. 5:8) Without holiness no one shall see the Lord. Without purity of heart no one will live in holiness. "Create in me a pure heart, O God, and renew a steadfast spirit within me." (Ps. 51:10) That is the cry of the repentant man who longs for the holiness of God in his life.

"Make a tree good and its fruit will be good, or make a tree bad and its fruit will be bad, for a tree is recognised by its fruit . . . For out of the overflow of the heart the mouth speaks. The good man brings good things out of the good stored up in him, and the evil man brings evil things out of the evil stored up in him." (Matt. 12:33–5)

The state of the heart conditions a person's words and actions as the heart of a tree will determine its fruitfulness. It may appear healthy, but if it is diseased at the heart, it will not be fruitful. Similarly, it is not people's appearance that betrays what is in their hearts, but what they say and do. "What comes out of a man is what makes him 'unclean'. For from within, out of men's hearts, come evil thoughts, sexual immorality, theft, murder, adultery, greed, malice, deceit, lewdness, envy, slander, arrogance and folly. All these evils come from inside and make a man 'unclean'." (Mark 7:20–23)

What a list! And it is by no means exhaustive. Jesus simply wants to make His point. We might want to excuse ourselves for our sins, blaming the circumstances, temptation, the past or other people. The plain truth is that all sin is conceived in the heart. We sin because, at heart, we want to sin and please ourselves.

There can be no doubting the necessity of asking God to purify our hearts. One of the ancient prayers of the Church is still used extensively at Holy Communion services: "Cleanse the thoughts of our hearts by the inspiration of your Holy Spirit."

Even the thoughts of our hearts are not right. How often do we find ourselves thinking unlovingly about others? How often do we give way to fantasies that have self at the centre, allowing our imaginations to project us into the centre of ungodly situations? How often do we react wrongly to others? How often do we put on an appearance of godliness, while within there is rage, bitterness, jealousy, sulking, pride or selfishness longing to be expressed?

The word "heart" can signify different things in Scripture. It can refer to the seat of the affections, to our emotions. Others can touch us in that area of our being. But it refers also to the human spirit that God alone can touch with His divine power, and that influences the affections, the mind, the will and ultimately what we do with our bodies.

By the sanctifying work of His Spirit, God is constantly dealing with us at heart level. He wants to see purity of motive and intention; purity of thought and action. The man who wants God's purposes in his life is not afraid to ask the Lord to deal with his heart, to reveal where there is impurity, deceit and wickedness stored up in him. He can easily be deceived about the state of his own heart, and God allows adverse circumstances to demonstrate to him what he would otherwise be blind to.

The way of purity is the way of love, "which comes from a pure heart and a good conscience and a sincere faith". (1 Tim 1:5) He tells Timothy to "pursue righteousness, faith, love and peace, along with those who call on the Lord out of a pure heart". (2 Tim. 2:22)

Here again is the paradox. It is only because God has put His love into our hearts that we desire to please Him, to walk in righteousness and have the purity of mind and holiness of life He desires for us. And yet we are conscious of so many things that belong to the old life, fighting against that purity. Is there any answer to this predicament?

Yes, there is, and the Lord has given the answer to every believer; it is his or hers already. That answer is the Holy Spirit: God's Holy Presence living within us. Holiness is allowing His Spirit to lead, guide, teach, inspire, fill, enable us in every situation. There is nothing impure about Him and He will never lead us into impure ways.

Paul prayed for the Philippians, "And this is my prayer: that your love may abound more and more in knowledge and depth of insight, so that you may be able to discern what is best and may be pure and blameless until the day of Christ, filled with the fruit of righteousness that comes

through Jesus Christ – to the glory and praise of God."
(Phil. 1:9–11)

Allow God the Holy Spirit to show you the hidden
desires, motives and intentions in your heart that displease
Him and hinder you. Remember, the heart is deceitful
above all things, so you will need the light of Jesus to reveal
what you cannot see for yourself.

Be encouraged that the Lord wants to reveal more of
Himself to you and holds out to you the glorious hope that
you will see Him, and when you do, His transforming work
in your life will be complete: you will be like Him.

Blessed are the pure in heart, for they will see God.

THE GREAT PROMISE

"They shall see God": that is the hope of every Christian
and when we see Him as He is we shall be like Him; God's
sanctifying work in our lives will be complete.

There is a sense in which we are to see the fulfilment of
these words in our present circumstances, as well as our
future hope. Those with pure hearts will readily draw near
to God in prayer, entering the Most Holy Place. There they
will know His presence and see something of His glory.
What they see will only be a tiny foretaste of what is to
come, but enough to encourage them to remain faithful and
true to the end.

The writer to the Hebrews is adamant about the need to
keep looking Godwards: "Therefore, holy brothers who
share in the heavenly calling, fix your thoughts on Jesus, the
apostle and high priest we confess." (Heb. 3:1) There is
constant temptation to concentrate on ourselves instead of
Him, to be over-concerned about our own needs and
dilemmas. The more we look in upon ourselves the more
confused and discouraged we become. That is why the
introverted person finds it difficult to walk in faith.

We grow in holiness, not by seeking out every shred of
unholiness, but by looking away from ourselves to the holy

Lord. His Spirit will bring before us those impurities of heart we would never discover by our own digging and delving. If we keep looking to Jesus we will know the cleansing of those impurities and we will know Him more clearly: "Let us then approach the throne of grace with confidence, so that we may receive mercy and find grace to help us in our time of need." (Heb. 4:16)

We must never lose sight of our nothingness before God, but He does not want us to concentrate on our unworthiness but on His worthiness by which we are made worthy.

You can keep your eyes on your weakness, failure and fear and be rendered useless to the Kingdom. What faith you have will be inactive as you will be so aware of your futility. However, if in your uselessness you look away from yourself, humbling yourself before Jesus and fixing your eyes on Him, then you will find the level of faith rising within you. You will remember that He has accepted you in your weakness and futility so that in Him you might find strength and power to do the impossible; "Let us draw near to God with a sincere heart and full assurance of faith." (Heb. 10:22)

The Holy Spirit makes you aware of what you are, only to lead you to Jesus and make you aware of who He is.

I AM WHO I AM

When God spoke to Moses from the burning bush, he answered, "Here I am." The Lord tells him to return to Egypt to lead the Israelites out of bondage. Moses pleads: "Who am I, that I should go to Pharaoh and bring the Israelites out of Egypt?" He is aware of his total inadequacy for the task.

The Lord's answer is to assure him "I will be with you." If Moses looks to Him he will have nothing to fear. Even this assurance is not enough. What is Moses to say to the people if they question him on what authority he is acting? God replies: "I AM WHO I AM. This is what you are to say to the Israelites: 'I AM has sent me to you'." (Ex. 3:14)

It is not what Moses is that matters, but who God is and what He is capable of. "By faith he left Egypt, not fearing the king's anger; he persevered because he saw him who is invisible." (Heb. 11:27) Moses prevailed because he kept his eyes on the Lord. The one occasion when he listened to men rather than God resulted in him seeing the Promised Land but not being allowed to enter it.

What an encouragement for us to keep our eyes fixed on Jesus: "Let us fix our eyes on Jesus, the author and perfector of our faith . . . Consider him who endured such opposition from sinful men, so that you will not grow weary and lose heart." (Heb. 12:2,3)

Whenever you are tempted to look at yourself, your own thoughts and desires; whenever you feel self-pity or self-concern, turn away from yourself and look to the Lord. As you ask for His forgiveness and purity of heart so your awareness of who Jesus is and of His presence with you will carry you through the situation with triumphant faith rather than dismal failure: "Since then, you have been raised with Christ, set your hearts on things above, where Christ is seated at the right hand of God. Set your minds on things above, not on earthly things. For you died, and your life is now hidden with Christ in God. When Christ, who is your life, appears, then you also will appear with him in glory." (Col. 3:1–4)

It is not who you are that is of great significance, but who God is, the great I AM who has made you His own. It is in Him that you live and move and have your being.

I am who I am.

FUTURE HOPE

"They shall see God" is also the glorious promise, the future hope, for all who remain faithful and true to the Lord. Beyond this life we shall see Him clearly for who He is and then, we are promised, we shall be like Him. That is a miracle far beyond anything we can imagine or experience now. Then we shall be able to reflect His glory far more perfectly than could be the case during our earthly existence. "Then the righteous will shine like the sun in the kingdom of their Father." (Matt. 13:43)

That will be the moment of complete satisfaction. David writes: "And I – in righteousness I will see your face; when I awake I will be satisfied with seeing your likeness." (Ps. 17:15) That is the fulfilment of the greatest aspiration of any Christian believer; to behold the face of the one he has loved. "You will fill me with joy in your presence, with eternal pleasures at your right hand." (Ps. 16:11)

We shall be able to stand the vision of the heavenly King, whose eyes are "like blazing fire" (Rev. 1:14) only because we come washed in the blood of Jesus, clothed in His righteousness, the children of His grace.

PEACEMAKERS

God wants us to live with the awareness of the privileges we have as His sons. The man of God will not be content with his status as a son; he will want to live up to that status, to demonstrate the stature of his sonship. Jesus said: "Blessed are the peacemakers, for they will be called sons of God."

A person becomes a son when he has made his peace with God. He has experienced reconciliation with God through the blood of Jesus, has received new life and is a new creation: "If anyone is in Christ, he is a new creation; the old has gone, the new has come! All this is from God, who reconciled us to himself through Christ and gave us the ministry of reconciliation: that God was reconciling the world to himself in Christ, not counting men's sins against them." (2 Cor. 5:17–19)

A true son has a deep desire to influence the lives of others who need to know God and be brought into fellowship with Him. Having made his peace with God, he wants to lead others to the Cross that they too might know His peace. He becomes a peacemaker, sharing in Christ's own ministry of reconciliation. "And he has committed to us this message of reconciliation. We are therefore Christ's ambassadors, as though God were making his appeal through us – we implore you on Christ's behalf: Be reconciled to God. God made him who had no sin to be sin for us, so that in him we might become the righteousness of God." (2 Cor. 5:19–21)

In Scripture, a son is to reflect the life of his Father. So a son of God will want to manifest the righteousness, holiness, purity of heart, faith and love of his Father. The sons of God are those who are led by the Spirit of God, following obediently in the way that He sets before them. "The mind controlled by the Spirit is life and peace." (Rom. 8:6)

The effectiveness of a Christian's witness depends on his personal obedience to his heavenly Father. The believer who wants to be a peacemaker will need to remain at peace with God. If he strays into sin, the witness of the Holy Spirit within him causes him to lose his peace. This is like a warning signal that he has grieved God and needs to be reconciled again to Him.

Others need to see in you the deep inner peace which is beyond understanding and that the world cannot give, so that they may be drawn to the Lord who alone can give such peace. But you will not be at peace with God unless you are also at peace with others. No matter what is done to you or said about you by someone else, you need to maintain an attitude of forgiveness and continue to hold out your hand in fellowship.

Unity is precious to the Lord. Use the opportunities you are given to lead others to be reconciled with one another – in the church fellowship, in marriage, at work. Jesus prayed: "May they be brought to complete unity to let the world know that you sent me and have loved them even as you have loved me." (John 17:23)

That love of unity is an essential part of holiness; division, enmity and strife a denial of it. That does not mean that you will always succeed in your attempts to bring reconciliation, but be willing to take the initiative in attempting to do so. "If it is possible, as far as it depends on you, live at peace with everyone." (Rom. 12:18)

That work of reconciliation may need to begin in your home, with your wife or children. It may be that tension exists between yourself and others in the fellowship to which you belong, or with those you work with. You may think you were not at fault or are to blame, that you did not initiate the difficulties that have arisen. You may be waiting for others to take the initiative to bring about reconciliation. It may seem that nothing positive can happen until the others recognise their faults and ask for your forgiveness. Jesus says you are to take the initiative: "If your brother sins against you, go and show him his fault, just between the two of you. If he listens to you, you have won your brother over." (Matt. 18:15)

Before you go to him make sure that your motive is to express genuine love for him, that there is no judgment or anger in your attitude. It is better to begin by confessing your negative reaction to him and asking for his forgiveness, than to be critical of him. Then he may see his sin before you have to point it out. If it is necessary to show him his fault obey what Jesus tells you to do remembering that your purpose is to be a peacemaker, not demonstrate self-righteousness.

Such times of reconciliation are seldom easy, but are vitally necessary and can lead to deeper unity than before. To delay facing the situation only prolongs the tension and increases the difficulty of finding true reconciliation.

You will not be able to spread peace around you if you are full of tension and anxiety. The Lord has called you to a life of faith and the man who puts his trust in Him will live in peace.

Peace was Jesus' parting gift to His disciples: "Peace I leave with you; my peace I give you. Do not let your hearts be troubled and do not be afraid." (John 14:27)

Paul begins his letters with the greeting: "Grace and peace to you from God our Father and the Lord Jesus Christ." (1 Cor. 1:3) "He himself is our peace," he tells the Ephesians. (2:14) "Let the peace of Christ rule in your hearts, since as members of one body you were called to peace." (Col. 3:15)

It is the God of peace who will sanctify you through and through. The more His peace is at work within you, the less anxious you will be and the more able to be a peacemaker. For peacemakers reflect something of the life of Jesus and will be called sons of God; others will recognise them as such for their attitudes will contrast sharply with those of the world, where hurt is met with hurt, and where hearts are full of tension and anxiety.

Blessed are the peacemakers, for they will be called sons of God.

PERSECUTION

The believer soon discovers that not all want to live at peace with him. His lifestyle and beliefs are a challenge to those around him if he is seeking to live in the righteousness of God. Those who are living in unrighteousness will be convicted because of the example set by the faithful Christian, which is why Jesus was such a threat to the Scribes, Pharisees and other religious leaders of His day. Jesus said: "Blessed are those who are persecuted because of righteousness, for theirs is the kingdom of heaven." (Matt. 5:10)

We must expect persecution from the world because the ways of Jesus are so strikingly different from the world. In our unrighteous society there is a desperate need for living examples of righteousness – not self-righteous people withdrawing from the society in which they live, but those in whom the positive virtues of Jesus will be seen, taking His life into the world.

Much of the persecution faithful Christians encounter comes from within the structures of the churches, where righteousness is out of fashion and spiritual standards have fallen. Those who are not living righteously are immediately challenged by righteous living. Instead of responding positively with repentance some have no desire to humble themselves before God and seek His righteousness in their own lives. Instead they try to make life as uncomfortable for the obedient as they can. It is persecution within the Church that is so destructive of unity and effective witness.

Persecution from the world has always strengthened the Church, sifting out those who are serious about their commitment to Christ from those who pay Him lip-service. In many places local churches appear so lifeless there is little for the world to persecute.

STAND FIRM

The faithful are those who will stand firm in the face of opposition whether it comes from the world or within the churches. They know that the real battle is not against flesh and blood, but against the "spiritual forces of evil". They believe the promise of Jesus: "Blessed are you when people insult you, persecute you and falsely say all kinds of evil against you because of me. Rejoice and be glad, because great is your reward in heaven, for in the same way they persecuted the prophets who were before you." (Matt. 5:11–12)

Jesus Himself was persecuted and the one who decides to walk faithfully with Him is bound to share in the fellowship of His sufferings. Often it is not personal rejection that Christians encounter, but rejection of the One whom they represent in the world.

The Holy Spirit, by His presence within the believer, gives boldness and peace in the face of any opposition. To seek to live the life of the Kingdom on earth will meet with opposition from those who do not want the will of God in their lives. But the reward for living Kingdom life now is to know the joy of that heavenly Kingdom for eternity.

No wonder, then, that Jesus says the man persecuted for the sake of righteousness is blessed – "happy, to be envied, and spiritually prosperous (that is, with life – joy and salvation in God's favour and salvation, regardless of your outward conditions)". (Matt. 5:11, Amplified)

The rejection most believers encounter seems feeble

compared with that experienced by those imprisoned, tortured or even martyred for their faith. Would you remain faithful to the Lord in the face of such fierce opposition? Perhaps you fear you would fail. God always supplies the grace necessary for His children to stand firm. If you were placed in that kind of situation those resources of grace would be made available to you.

It is more relevant for you to face whatever persecution and rejection you experience now with positive, faithful attitudes, never compromising the truth by seeking to appease others. God will honour those who honour Him: "I tell you, whoever acknowledges me before men, the Son of Man will also acknowledge him before the angels of God. But he who disowns me before men will be disowned before the angels of God." (Luke 12:8–9)

Are there opportunities to witness that you have missed because you have feared the reaction if you were to do so? Has the Holy Spirit been prompting you to some particular action and you have stubbornly refused because you want everyone to think well of you? Is it not better to be obedient, even at cost to yourself, than to grieve the Lord?

Have you grown weary from having to remain faithful in a situation where there is continual opposition, misunderstanding or deliberate misrepresentation? "Consider him who endured such opposition from sinful men, so that you will not grow weary and lose heart." (Heb. 12:3)

Pray for the grace you need. God will not be slow in supplying all that is required to speak and act in His name – and to cope with any adverse reactions you encounter. Remember the inheritance God has promised you, "for our light and momentary troubles are achieving for us an eternal glory that far outweighs them all. So we fix our eyes not on what is seen, but on what is unseen. For what is seen is temporary, but what is unseen is eternal." (2 Cor. 4:17–18)

Blessed are those who are persecuted because of righteousness, for theirs is the kingdom of heaven.

16. RENEWAL OF THE MIND

Unholy thoughts plague most Christians. Critical, lustful or jealous thoughts are only the tip of an enormous iceberg. Many other things go on in their minds that they know are wrong and offensive to God. They may fight these thoughts but feel defeated by their persistence. Some they may enjoy but many they long to be rid of.

THE PROBLEM

Jesus said: "The eye is the lamp of the body. If your eyes are good, your whole body will be full of light." (Matt. 6:22) Those who want to see God's holiness in their lives are greatly disturbed by their lustful thoughts and fantasies. Mental images that encourage lust are imprinted on the mind by television, films, lurid books as well as attractive people. Once imprinted there it is difficult to be rid of them, and they drift to the surface when most unwanted.

Any pastor will know the distress of those who come seeking counsel when they are afflicted by blasphemous thoughts, often at the most holy of moments as, for example, when receiving Holy Communion.

Wandering thoughts are a common difficulty in prayer and worship. At the very moment when you most want to concentrate on the Lord your mind wanders on to all kinds of other topics, often trivial and irrelevant.

The Christian sometimes feels unable to refrain from expressing his proud thoughts. He may know that in humility he should keep silent; but he feels he has to defend himself, prove himself or belittle others. The remorse he feels afterwards does not hold him back.

Selfish thoughts abound and influence his actions all too often. He will serve, if it is convenient. He will help, if he can think of no good reason why he can be excused. Before undertaking anything he is likely to assess the consequences from a selfish point of view.

We put ourselves at the centre of great imaginings, projecting ourselves into positions of importance where others will respect and admire us. We daydream of ourselves being at the centre of great escapades. Obviously pride is at the root of such thoughts, but why should our minds wander in this way when we are wanting to concentrate on other and more important things? It seems we are not in complete control of our thoughts. We find ourselves thinking about one thing when we want to be thinking about something entirely different.

There may be times when you want to think positively about others and yet critical thoughts, or jealous and angry attitudes seem to flare up within you. Fear and suspicion are aroused instead of confidence and trust.

And then there are times when we feel totally confused in our thinking. God is not a God of confusion and we don't want to be confused, so it is perplexing to understand how this turmoil within us can persist.

At crucial moments, you can have a sudden loss of memory. Everything goes blank and you cannot recall the relevant facts you need. And there are all those negative, accusing thoughts that drain you of confidence and cause you to feel utterly condemned if you accept them. Depression can be caused by believing one negative thought after another until you are no longer able to think positively.

There are occasions when you feel urged to act impulsively without proper time to weigh the thought to determine whether it is from God. He does not compel us. He directs us, commands us, leads us; but He does not bypass our minds. He wants us to be in full control of our thinking, so that our minds can assess what He is saying by the Spirit and translate His Word into action.

The enemy loves Christians to be passive in their thinking, readily accepting any and every thought that comes into their minds. He feeds in his lies and the unwary will believe what he says, even though he completely contradicts God's Word. He enjoys disrupting their thinking, encouraging vain imaginings, impure and wandering thoughts.

Eastern forms of mysticism betray their satanic origins by encouraging passive attitudes. To attempt to empty your mind is to leave it vacant for the enemy to use and he will not miss the opportunity. Many of the devotees of such forms of prayer seem mindless almost; they have lost the capacity to use their minds actively.

The minds of Christians are prone to particular problems, such as prejudice. For centuries they have been divided by doctrinal positions and self-righteous attitudes. Close-minded prejudice prevents them from hearing one another, let alone learning from one another. When prejudice dominates a man, he will defend a position rather than seek the truth.

The passive attitudes of super-spiritual people give the impression that the Christian life is an endless Bible study. They bear little fruit, although they sound so spiritual when they speak. Satan encourages God's children to be unfruitful. The mind is his first line of attack. If he can influence their thinking, he can influence what they do, or fail to do.

WHY SUCH PROBLEMS?

At first sight it seems a depressing situation, with the enemy able to influence the minds of God's children in so many different ways. Why should this be? That question can only be answered by remembering our condition before conversion to Christ. The enemy has great control over the minds of unbelievers, blinding them to spiritual truths. "The god of this age has blinded the minds of unbelievers, so that they cannot see the light of the gospel of the glory of Christ, who is the image of God." (2 Cor. 4:4)

Before his conversion, a Christian believed that he was free to choose what to do with his life, his time, his money, his body even. "Once you were alienated from God and were enemies in your minds because of your evil behaviour." (Col. 1:21) His mind was conditioned for many years to live in opposition to God's holiness. He may have had a keen sense of morality and tried to live a "good, clean life". But still his unbelief betrays an opposition to God that would have affected his behaviour in many ways. He only has to consider how many of his attitudes, and hence his actions, have changed since knowing Jesus, to realise the truth of that.

God "gives over to a depraved mind" those who are adamant in their refusal to submit to His ways. The unspiritual man cannot understand the things that come from the Spirit of God, "but we have the mind of Christ". (1 Cor. 2:16) If that is true then how can the enemy still have access to the minds of Christians? They may have been in spiritual darkness once, blinded by the god of this age, but surely the light of Christ has now come into their lives to set them free from all such darkness?

To receive the light of Christ is not to be perfectly filled with light; there are still those areas of darkness where the Holy Spirit needs to bring the cleansing of Jesus.

Satan has no RIGHT to affect the mind of a Christian, but that does not prevent him from trying to do so. If he can control any aspect of thinking because his repentance has been incomplete he will do so. If the Christian places himself in positions of temptation because his flesh still desires to be sinfully employed, his mind is obviously involved in such activity.

THE ANSWER

Every Christian needs to know how to keep the conscious level of his mind clear of enemy activity. All the negativity, destructive, critical, sinful thoughts that he tries to put into the mind of the believer are like flaming arrows. Paul says:

"Take up the shield of faith, with which you can extinguish all the flaming arrows of the evil one." (Eph. 6:16)

This is something YOU have to do as a Christian. It is no use asking God to take these evil thoughts away from you. They do not come from Him. So you must deal with the one from whom they do come. It is YOU who must take up the shield of faith by rejecting the thought as soon as you are conscious of it. Say to yourself (or out loud if you are on your own), "I reject that thought in the name of Jesus." Immediately turn your mind on to the Lord and praise Him. You will need to do this again and again to keep the conscious level of your mind free from enemy activity and able to be more sensitive to the voice of God's Spirit.

You only dwell on evil thoughts if deep in your heart you want them. With the shield of faith you can "extinguish all the flaming arrows of the evil one". All of them. If you stand firm against the devil in his attempts to distract you he will flee from you.

Take up the shield of faith, with which you can extinguish all the flaming arrows of the evil one.

PULLING DOWN STRONGHOLDS

The enemy may be allowed to maintain certain strongholds in a believer's mind, from which he can readily try to affect his thinking and actions. Once those strongholds are removed, Satan cannot affect his thinking from within. But that will not prevent him from trying to cause disturbance from without. Many of the "flaming arrows" the enemy will throw at him will be thoughts to entice him into sin, encouraging wrong attitudes and actions.

If a Christian is constantly critical of others, the enemy has a stronghold in his thinking. Your mind will be full of lustful thoughts if you enjoy your lust and do not truly want God to deal with it. You will continue to be critical of others if you feel justified in your criticism and are proud of heart.

You will continue to be prejudiced if you are blind to your prejudice.

How do you deal with the strongholds once you truly want to be set free from the areas of thinking where the enemy is able to feed negative, destructive thoughts into your mind? "The weapons we fight with are not the weapons of the world. On the contrary, they have divine power to demolish strongholds. We demolish arguments and every pretension that sets itself up against the knowledge of God, and we take captive every thought to make it obedient to Christ." (2 Cor. 10:4–5)

There is our aim: to take captive every thought and make it obedient to Christ. God has given us spiritual weapons that have power to demolish the strongholds of the enemy, both in our own lives and in the world around us. Considerable vigilance is going to be needed if your mind is going to be cleansed of enemy activity.

To be cleansed of the strongholds in your thinking you need to repent of allowing the enemy to maintain these footholds in your mind and to want genuinely to be free from them. The enemy must not be allowed any ground to stand on, or any grounds to resist you.

Then, in the name of Jesus, take authority over the particular problem and order the enemy to depart immediately. You are not engaging in a battle; you are proclaiming the victory of Jesus that He has won for you on the Cross.

It is helpful to ask one or two others to agree with you in prayer. The enemy has no right to your mind so he will have to release that stronghold. This, however, does not stop him firing his "flaming arrows". Christians can easily be deceived into thinking the problem has not been properly dealt with simply by having a negative thought directed at them.

For example, if the person with a critical attitude has been freed through repentance, forgiveness and using the spiritual weapons at his disposal, he should not be surprised if he still experiences the temptation to think critically of others sometimes. He will be able to take the shield of faith against those thoughts. Having them does not mean that he is still bound by a critical attitude.

The importance of repentance in this whole matter cannot be emphasised enough. Without that, the victory of the Spirit over the flesh will not be established. And it may be necessary to ask the Spirit to reveal the nature of these strongholds. No one is more blind to his prejudice than a man with prejudice!

POSITIVE USE OF THE MIND

Acting against the negative will not be enough; our minds need to be set on the positive things of the Spirit. "The mind of sinful man is death, but the mind controlled by the Spirit is life and peace, because the sinful mind is hostile to God. It does not submit to God's law, nor can it do so. Those controlled by the sinful nature cannot please God." (Rom. 8:6–8)

If strongholds in the mind persist it is because the heart is not right. It may be that the Christian is excusing himself for his sin, blaming past experiences or other people, or pleading he is unable to resist the temptation. While he is excusing himself he will not be repentant.

Prayer will not change your fleshly thoughts into godly ones. Those thoughts will need to be resisted in the name of Jesus. Anything that is from God can be measured by His Word; so if there is uncertainty whether a particular thought is from God judge it by the Bible.

God will not take control of your mind; if He did you would become a mindless robot. He has made you in such a way that you are to control your mind and be able to submit it willingly to Him to be under the influence of the Holy Spirit. Your mind will only be renewed by using the spiritual weapons or resources God makes available to you.

It may be that you will need to do business with God until you come to the place where you can honestly say to Him that you are at fault, want forgiveness and need to be set free. It is common for people to seek ministry from others to deal with problems that stem from their own heart attitude towards the Lord. Ministry can never be a substitute for repentance. Any true ministry in the Spirit in this area will lead the person to acknowledge his need of repentance.

It may well be true that past experiences and environment have contributed towards an area of bondage in a person's mind. That may be the cause, but not the remedy. The answer is the Cross and the blood of Jesus shed to free us from all sin. Even when the Spirit makes it clear that it is important to recognise the cause, healing can only happen by coming with repentance to the Cross.

PROPER USE OF THE MIND

The sinful mind was hostile to God and would not submit to Him. Repentance involves a change of mind followed by a proper use of the mind. "Those who live in accordance with the Spirit have their minds set on what the Spirit desires." (Rom. 8:5)

"Set your mind on things above, not on earthly things." (Col. 3:2) What does that mean in practice? "Finally, brothers, whatever is true, whatever is noble, whatever is right, whatever is pure, whatever is lovely, whatever is admirable – if anything is excellent or praiseworthy – think about such things." (Phil. 4:8)

After years of blindness due to unbelief, the mind of the Christian needs to be re-programmed. It is so used to being set on proud and selfish motives, on things that would satisfy the flesh, such as the objects of lust or greed; it is so accustomed to reacting with self-righteous criticism and judgment, that it is not easy to learn to concentrate on what is good and wholesome. But this is essential if we are to have renewed minds and know the will of God in our lives: "Do not conform any longer to the pattern of this world, but be transformed by the renewing of your mind. Then you will be able to test and approve what God's will is – his good, pleasing and perfect will." (Rom. 12:2)

The renewing of our minds brings a transformation to our lives and is part of God's sanctifying work. Just as the blood of Jesus cleanses our minds from the rubbish, so the Spirit encourages us to set them on things above. The Word of God needs to dwell in our minds richly. When we praise God we look away from ourselves to He who is holy and pure in every one of His thoughts.

The Lord does not want us to try and hide our thoughts from Him in shame, but to expose them to His light, so that His sanctifying power may continue to be at work in us. As we set our minds on what God wants, we are less conscious of our own earthly desires that would be in conflict with Him. We want what He wants.

Again, the right motivation is a great asset here. Those engaged in ministry to others know how important it is for them to be mentally attuned to the Spirit if they are going to be effective in that ministry. It is impossible to know the mind of the Spirit clearly if they are allowing their minds to be filled with rubbish.

The same principle is true of all Christians, for they all need to know the leading of the Spirit in their lives. No wonder many find it difficult to know the voice of God if they are indisciplined in the use of their minds, allowing them to be set on all kinds of ungodly things. We do well to remember that Jesus told us to love God with all our heart, mind and strength. When we concentrate on the positive we lose interest in the negative. And God is positive; His Word is positive; the Holy Spirit is positive.

Those who live in accordance with the Spirit have their minds set on what the Spirit desires.

17. FAITHFUL LOVE

Loving is giving. To love God with all the heart is to give yourself wholeheartedly to Him withholding nothing. "Love must be sincere. Hate what is evil; cling to what is good. Be devoted to one another in brotherly love. Honour one another above yourselves. Never be lacking in zeal, but keep your spiritual fervour, serving the Lord." (Rom. 12:9–11)

There is as much in the New Testament about our relationships with one another as about our relationship with God. The one is reflected in the other. Love is not an abstract concept; it is expressed in giving and serving in practical ways.

Everyone needs to be loved, accepted and appreciated. Words that express love are not enough; the love needs to be seen in positive action. Your love is put to the test whenever the Lord puts before you a need that He wants you to meet.

How many pastors have experienced the frustration of encouraging their people to open their homes to those in need of love, only to be met with excuse after excuse? It is inconvenient for one reason or another. By contrast there are those who do not mind how much inconvenience they may suffer so long as they know they are obeying God's Word and expressing love to His people. "Let no debt remain outstanding, except the continuing debt to love one another, for he who loves his fellow man has fulfilled the law." (Rom. 13:8)

LOVE IS PRACTICAL

In practical ways God will call on us to share His love with others. The flesh does not like cost. We would prefer to choose who we give to and when. The super-spiritual people, always full of the right words but with little positive action, will delay responding to need. That gives time to think of excuses for not acting, or, hopefully, for the problem or need to disappear.

Faith is not expressed by inactivity when God is telling you to get on with a job! It is seen when you step out in obedience, believing that the Lord will supply all the grace and power required to see the need met. "Then the King will say to those on his right, 'Come, you who are blessed by my Father; take your inheritance, the kingdom prepared for you since the creation of the world. For I was hungry and you gave me something to eat, I was thirsty and you gave me something to drink. I was a stranger and you invited me in, I needed clothes and you clothed me, I was sick and you looked after me, I was in prison and you came to visit me . . . I tell you the truth, whatever you did for one of the least of these brothers of mine, you did for me.'" (Matt. 25:34–6,40)

The "righteous" are unaware of the way in which they give to the Lord, because it is second nature to them to give, to love, to serve others. They don't hesitate to wonder whether it is convenient. They get on with what they know God is asking them to do. When people came to Jesus for help, He did not respond by telling them He must pray about whether it was right for Him to help!

"The spirit is willing, but the body is weak" (Matt. 26:41) is a text quoted and misused on numerous occasions. The body is often weak because the heart is unwilling. It is one thing to find it difficult to do something we want to do, quite another to feel tired because we are asked to do something we do not truly want to face!

It was the Pharisees and other religious leaders who were looking for the legalistic loopholes that would prevent them from facing what it means to give, love and serve. Jesus "looked round at them in anger" and was "deeply distressed at their stubborn hearts". (Mark 3:5) The parable of the Good Samaritan ends with the words, "Go and do likewise" when the legal expert said that the one who did the will of God was the one who showed mercy.

And that is what God expects of His children; "Whoever does God's will is my brother and sister and mother." (Mark 3:35) However, we can never outdo the Lord in giving: "Consider carefully what you hear," he continued. "With the measure you use, it will be measured to you – and even more. Whoever has will be given more; whoever does not have, even what he has will be taken from him." (Mark 4:24–5)

Your love for God will be expressed in the way you relate to your fellow Christians and in the way you serve others by giving to them. Do you resent it when people demand of you? Are you protective about your time, money, home? Do you regard these as your own, or do they belong to the Lord? Do you rejoice at the opportunities God gives you to meet the needs of others or do you resent them as intrusions in your life? When you do respond positively is it with the right motive, or are you looking for praise from others? Do you expect to be thanked and appreciated for what you do? "So you also, when you have done everything you were told to do, should say, 'We are unworthy servants; we have only done our duty.'" (Luke 17:10)

Jesus came among us as a servant, expressing His humble and loving attitude by washing the disciples' feet, normally the work of a slave. There are many ways in which He washes our feet, cleansing us, loving us, serving us, ministering to us. He asks only that we love and serve others as He loves and serves us: "I have set you an example that you should do as I have done to you. I tell you the truth, no servant is greater than his master, nor is a messenger greater than the one who sent him. Now that you know these things, you will be blessed if you do them." (John 13:15–17)

Your Master, Jesus, was prepared to humble Himself to serve regardless of the cost. You are not greater than He. His new commandment is: "Love one another. As I have loved you, so you must love one another. All men will know that you are my disciples if you love one another." (John 13:35) It is not love and service without holiness that the Lord requires of you, but love and service that is an expression of holiness.

Whatever you did for one of the least of these brothers of mine, you did for me.

HIS LOVE IN US

Jesus prayed to the Father, "that the love you have for me may be in them and that I myself may be in them." (John 17:26) This is an amazing request.

Jesus lived out His own teaching; there was no credibility gap between what He said and did. He gave Himself constantly to the people as He preached, taught and healed. "When they hurled their insults at him, he did not retaliate; when he suffered, he made no threats. Instead, he entrusted himself to him who judges justly." (1 Pet. 2:23)

We cannot understand the love that gives so freely, suffers such rejection and yet goes on giving, absorbing all the hurts, all the sins and fears of men, only to bless in return, showing mercy, compassion, patience and forgiveness. Yet it is that love which we see in Jesus and that God wants to see in us.

How different from human love and affection. When men are hurt their natural instinct is to retaliate and demand vengeance. When we are opposed we express indignation and immediately want to justify ourselves. We so often respond to others with jealousy, anger, bitterness or resentment. How unholy! How different from Jesus!

Our reactions to others reveal where we truly are spiritually. We can be guarded about our words and actions when we are seeking to impress others or want their approval, when we are anticipating difficulties or opposition. When the unexpected happens, whether through a trying situation or person, our first reaction reveals the true attitude of the heart. We may learn to hide that reaction, to bring our feelings under control and then respond as a Christian should. However, the Lord wants to purify our hearts in such a way that even the initial response to the situation reflects the holy love of Jesus.

Jesus prayed for the Father's love for Him to be in us. In other words He wants us to love Jesus as perfectly as the Father does.

The Father was always faithful to Jesus. When He commanded the wind and the waves, they were stilled. When He gave thanks over the five loaves and two fish they fed a multitude of thousands. When He called Lazarus to come out of the tomb, he was restored to life. When He prayed for the sick, they were healed. When He took authority over evil spirits, people were delivered. When He forgave sins, lives were gloriously transformed. When He went obediently to the Cross, He was raised from the dead. When He ascended, He reigned in heaven. Why? Because of the Father's great love for Him.

The Father honoured the words of Jesus, answered His prayers, miraculously intervened in the laws of nature, watched over Him as He suffered the ultimate act of consecration and raised Him in triumph. In all those activities we see the Father's love for the Son. We see His faithfulness to Him.

Jesus wants to see in us the holy love that will cause us to be entirely faithful to Him. The Father never let Jesus down. If we love Him with the perfect love of the Father neither shall we. That love HAS been given us in the gift of the Holy Spirit.

Jesus promised: "You will receive power when the Holy Spirit comes on you; and you will be my witnesses." (Acts 1:8) God needs to have a holy witness in the world, a people who love Jesus and are ready to obey Him; a people filled with His faith and power, ready to believe Him to do mighty things for the glory of His name.

Lack of love expresses unholiness. So does unbelief!

FAITH FOR GREAT THINGS

Jesus died on the Cross to make us holy, His blood can rid us of doubt and His Spirit can inspire faith in His Word to accomplish mighty things: "I tell you the truth, anyone who has faith in me will do what I have been doing. He will do even greater things than these, because I am going to the Father." (John 14:12)

Jesus used the phrase "I tell you the truth" when He knew what He was about to say would be met with unbelief. There are few verses of the New Testament that are received with more unbelief than this one! And yet Jesus is speaking of every true believer, "anyone who has faith".

What follows can be regarded both as a statement of fact and a promise. The believer will do what Jesus has been doing. Perhaps we want to limit that to mean we will live godly lives reflecting something of the character of Jesus. However, He is speaking about miracles in the context in which these words appear and obviously is referring to demonstrable works of power.

The believer will do even greater things than were possible in the earthly ministry of Jesus because the Holy Spirit had not been poured out freely on God's people at that time. When He returned to the Father, He prayed for the Spirit to be given to them. It is the Spirit who inspires faith in God's word and teaches us to trust Him to do the impossible.

To say that God no longer wants to act in such ways, that miracles ceased with the apostolic age, is a convenient cover for personal doubt. Such doubt is an aspect of unholiness; it does not reflect the faith of Jesus or obedience to His Word. He tells us that if we have faith the size of a mustard seed mountains will be moved, that He is willing to answer our prayers of faith and give us anything for which we ask in His name.

FAITHFULNESS

We see the faithfulness of God towards Jesus in that respect and He extends that same faithfulness to us as His children. "The work of God is this: to believe in the one he has sent." (John 6:29) All that is not of faith is sin and without faith it is impossible to please God.

In Scripture faith and love are not put in tension; they are complementary. "The only thing that counts," Paul tells the Galatians, "is faith expressing itself through love." (5:6) The Father honours such faith: "I tell you the truth, my Father will give you whatever you ask in my name." (John 16:23)

Know that God will always be faithful to you. He will never leave you, fail you or forsake you. His love for you will be steadfast and unchanging. That is the way He wants you to love Jesus, that you will prove faithful to the end and receive the crown of life.

Jesus has entrusted the life of His Holy Spirit to you; your body is a temple of His holy presence. He wants to see His life, His faith and love, expressed in you. He wants you to be reliable and dependable, a faithful witness. Others will be able to take you at your word as you can take Him at His. You will not let them down and have a bad reputation for making empty promises. It will be known you can be trusted. You won't make popular decisions, but the right ones. You won't tell people you love them without being prepared to back those words with positive action.

The only thing that counts is faith expressing itself in love.

18. HOLY GIVING

The widow who put her last coins into the Temple treasury was expressing holiness in her love for the Lord and willingness to entrust herself to Him. Out of her poverty she gave all that she had. That is holy faith, wholehearted trust in the Lord.

In our poverty we trust in the riches of Jesus. Faith is an essential dimension of holiness, manifesting the faith Jesus had in His Father, the faith expressed in going to the Cross trusting He would be raised. Only by entrusting ourselves wholeheartedly to God do we discover His power, not only to raise us to new life in Him, but also to release us into the ministries He has for us.

A ministry that does not demand a stretching of one's faith is a ministry sadly lacking in the anointing of God, for He is always wanting to extend His children, to see more of their potential realised. It is faithless to believe we lack potential or have reached the limit of the ways in which God would work through us.

FAITH EXPRESSED IN LOVE

The boldness of faith required in the purposes of God involves entrusting ourselves to the Lord as that widow did, knowing that He will not fail any of His children. It is pouring out what is costly for us to the Lord; "A woman came with an alabaster jar of very expensive perfume, made of pure nard. She broke the jar and poured the perfume on his head." (Mark 14:3)

There is no fear in love, no fear in faith, no fear in holiness; only a willingness to give oneself freely to God in whatever way the situation demands. These two women gave in very different ways: one offering her last coins to God, the other anointing Jesus with expensive ointment. Both are expressing their love and faith in the Lord.

Faith is expressed in the giving of ourselves, our time, abilities, money to God; it is unholy and unfaithful to withhold from him what is rightfully His, and invites Him to shut heaven in our faces. "You are under a curse – the whole nation of you – because you are robbing me. Bring the whole tithe into the storehouse, that there may be food in my house. Test me in this," says the Lord Almighty, "and see if I do not throw open the floodgates of heaven and pour out so much blessing that you will not have room enough for it." (Mal. 3:9–10)

The Lord tells us to test Him in this; He knows that we will not find Him unfaithful or lacking in generosity. Many believers today are discovering the rich blessings that God pours into their lives because they are faithful in their financial giving. That is a demonstration of their willingness to trust God. Several churches have experienced considerable renewal through learning to give money away instead of begging for it. What an unholy example churches give to the world by raising money. Our God is rich in every way and is revealed as the Lord our Provider; He will always provide for the work of His Kingdom.

However, it requires trust to believe He will provide. The faithless attitude suggests we do not have enough for our own needs, and therefore cannot afford to give away. That is inviting further poverty for the individual or church concerned. The Lord requires us to give, and then promises He will provide, not the other way round. Faith is not required if we wait for Him to provide and then give away some of what He has made available.

The minimum requirement of the Law is to give the Lord the tithe, the FIRST tenth of all you receive. The free-will offering is over and above that first tenth which is His by right.

In the New Testament, giving is to be MORE generous, not

less, for the Christian acknowledges that all he is and has belongs to the Lord. The faithful Christian will give a tithe – and more – to the Lord. That is holy giving. Material circumstances do not affect his need to do this, whether a child, a worker or a pensioner. He will seek an increase in faith so he can give more than the minimum requirement, knowing that the Lord will honour such faith: "With the measure you use, it will be measured to you – and even more." (Mark 4:24)

Some denominations have served their members badly by suggesting that all expenses should be deducted from income – rent, mortgage, rates, tax, food bills, heating etc. – before deciding what proportion of the remainder should be given to the Lord. This is to invite both spiritual and material poverty.

Even in the Old Testament, the FIRST tenth belonged to the Lord and that was a tenth of ALL that was received. God requires no less today and desires even more so He can "throw open the floodgates of heaven and pour out so much bl _ing that you will not have room enough for it."

FULFILLING THE LAW

When Christians do not want to face something in God's Word, they often challenge: "That is being legalistic." Jesus said: "I tell you the truth, until heaven and earth disappear, not the smallest letter, not the least stroke of a pen, will by any means disappear from the Law until everything is accomplished." (Matt. 5:18)

God has given us His Spirit so that the holy requirements of the Law can be fulfilled in our lives. Without the gift of the Spirit it was impossible to keep the demands the Law made upon people's lives. Now God has put His life into us to enable us to obey Him.

Some will want to protest and say they live by grace, not by law. They will quote Paul: "If you are led by the Spirit, you are not under law." (Gal 5:18) And that is right, because if we are led by the Spirit we do not need to have our lives regulated by a legalistic code or system. If we are led by the Spirit we will fulfil the Law without that being laid upon us as a burden.

So in the matter of tithing, for example, if we are led by the Spirit, we will be led to fulfil God's Word: we will give the first tenth, not as a legalistic obligation, but from a heart of love. We will rejoice to give to the Lord we love and to honour His commands, which are not burdensome. "Remember this: Whoever sows sparingly will also reap sparingly, and whoever sows generously will also reap generously. Each man should give what he has decided in his heart to give, not reluctantly or under compulsion, for God loves a cheerful giver. And God is able to make all grace abound to you, so that in all things at all times, having all that you need, you will abound in every good work." (2 Cor. 9:6–8)

God's purpose is not to take from us but to give to us, "so that in all things at all times, having all that you need, you will abound in every good work." He tells us to test Him in this matter of giving and receiving and He will not fail us.

Do not be misled into thinking that this is an optional aspect of the holiness of God in our lives. Paul continued by saying: "Now he who supplies seed to the sower and bread for food will also supply and increase your store of seed and will enlarge the harvest of your righteousness." (2 Cor. 9:10)

If you are truly concerned about the holiness of God in your life, will you not want the "harvest of your righteousness" to be increased? You are giving what is already God's anyway. It is He who supplies the seed.

WHERE TO GIVE

We need to be led of the Spirit so that we give WHERE the Lord wants us to give, as well as WHAT he wants to give. The New Testament gives no clear direction on this point, except that it is given to the work of the Lord, to support the ministry of preaching the Gospel, to share with any in need and to be responsible for the poor. Obviously, the Christian will give to his local fellowship. However, any farmer knows that it is a waste of time putting even the finest quality seed into barren soil. So the believer will need to be sensitive to the voice of the Spirit to ensure that he is giving WHERE it is right, supporting ministries that are anointed and used of God to truly build up the lives of Christians within the Body of Christ and ministries that are effective in evangelism and caring for the poor and needy of the world. If you are faithful in your giving, "You will be made rich in every way so that you can be generous on every occasion, and through us your generosity will result in thanksgiving to God." (2 Cor. 9:11)

A minister, newly appointed to a church in grave financial difficulty, taught his people the scriptural principles of giving. They began to apply this word to their own lives and the church finances. As promised, the Lord prospered them. Not only did the church income increase steadily so that they were able to give away more, but spiritual renewal also took place among the people.

Many gifts from beyond the members were given to the church, and faithfully every gift was tithed, the money being given away to evangelistic and missionary work. At first the gifts were of a few dollars, then hundreds and, as they proved faithful in their tithing, of a few thousand.

Then they were given a gift of $200,000. A tenth, $20,000, needed to be given away. At this the lay leadership baulked. How could they simply give away such a sum? And what were they to do with the rest of such a large gift? They decided to invest it so that the interest would pay their church expenses. They would not listen to their minister's protests, neither to the Lord's words: "Do not store up for yourselves treasures on earth . . . but store up for yourselves treasures in heaven . . . For where your treasure is, there will your heart be also." (Matt. 6:19,21)

The minister left that church grieved; the anointing also left and the faith and vitality of the people evaporated. God's way of faith, holiness and obedience are always best!

"Men will praise God for the obedience that accompanies your confession of the gospel of Christ, and for your generosity in sharing with them and with everyone else." (2 Cor. 9:13)

The ways of faith are contrary to the ways of the world. The work of the Gospel is hindered when people say they do not have the financial resources to do the things God lays on their hearts. He is always prepared to supply the resources to accomplish whatever He asks of us. That is true of money as it is of other resources. However, because the way of holiness is the way of faith, it is necessary to trust God for His provision. Without that trust the work falters and Christians sink to the degrading position of supporting the life of the congregation with jumble sales and garden fêtes. May God forgive His people for such unholiness. Does that give a powerful witness of God's love, care and provision for His people? He will make sure that gifts for His work flow where there are those who are willing to be faithful and obedient. "From the fullness of His grace we have all received one blessing after another." (John 1:16)

Whoever sows sparingly will also reap sparingly, and whoever sows generously will also reap generously.

19. A HOLY CHURCH

The world is not impressed by the witness of an unholy congregation. The words should be a contradiction in terms. When Paul begins his letters, he usually points his readers to their holy state; they are saints, God's holy, "set apart" people: "To all in Rome who are loved by God and called to be saints." (Rom. 1:7) They are called to live up to their high calling as those loved by God.

"To the church of God in Corinth, to those sanctified in Christ Jesus and called to be holy." (1 Cor. 1:2) Here Paul speaks of what Jesus has accomplished. They are already sanctified in God's sight and are called, therefore, to be holy in character and living.

"To the saints in Ephesus, the faithful in Christ Jesus." (Eph. 1:1) Saints are not restricted to those canonised by some denominations. Every believer is made a saint through Jesus and God requires him or her to live faithfully as such. "To the holy and faithful brothers in Christ at Colossae." (Col. 1:2)

Men would not continue in their sinful, rebellious and disobedient ways if they knew the majesty and glory of God. Bound by sin and in the grip of evil they could not bear the revelation of His holiness; they would be destroyed. Only those washed with the blood of the Lamb, Jesus, can truly meet with God in His holiness. Washed in that blood they can meet with God without feeling condemned by the encounter, although full of awe at His splendour and majesty, and the wonder of His love in revealing Himself to those who deserve nothing from Him.

The Holy Spirit comes upon Christians to lead them to the holiness of God. When they first encounter the Holy Spirit, they will be aware of great differences taking place in their lives. And yet there may be little "brokenness" about their Christian lives. That leads to some strange situations.

Within the institutional churches there are many who have not come to a personal relationship with the Lord Jesus Christ, to a heartfelt love for Him that motivates them for a life of true discipleship and obedience. There are many others who have a personal faith, experience the love of the Holy Spirit being poured into their lives, but who lose their initial enthusiasm to please God.

In Paul's letter to Ephesus he speaks of great spiritual truths that have been an inspiration to the Church throughout her history. Yet here, only a few years later, the Spirit is warning the same church of the need to repent, to turn back to God, to seek again the love and power that is needed to be His faithful witness. If the Christians do not respond to the warning they will fall even further from the Lord's grace and favour.

SARDIS

To live in holiness a Christian needs to be filled to overflowing with God's Holy Spirit. The same is true for any congregation that is going to please the Lord; the power of His holy presence in the midst of His people needs to be overwhelming. To Sardis he says; "I know your deeds; you have a reputation of being alive, but you are dead. Wake up! Strengthen what remains, and is about to die, for I have not found your deeds complete in the sight of my God. Remember, therefore, what you have received and heard; obey it, and repent. But if you do not wake up, I will come like a thief, and you will not know at what time I will come to you." (Rev. 3:1–3)

Reputations are not enough; it is the life manifested that counts. It does not matter what a congregation claims for itself. How much of Jesus is seen in the worship, the ministry and relationships of those people? That is what concerns the Lord. Are they a people concerned to live holy lives so the Kingdom of God may be extended in that place?

We do not want Him to say of us what He said of His people of old: "All day long I have held out my hands to an obstinate people, who walk in ways not good, pursuing their own imaginations – a people who continually provoke me to my very face." (Is. 65:2–3)

Although His hatred of sin is great, God's love for sinners is wonderful. Jesus said: "I have not come to call the righteous, but sinners." (Matt. 9:13) We need never fear to face what we are, so long as we are prepared to come to Him humbly and allow Him to cleanse us and refine us. "Come to me, all you who are weary and burdened, and I will give you rest. Take my yoke upon you and learn from me, for I am gentle and lowly in heart, and you will find rest for your souls. For my yoke is easy and my burden is light." (Matt. 11:28–30)

Yet this same Jesus who came to give His life for sinners and to take our burdens upon Himself, also tells us: "If your hand or your foot causes you to sin, cut if off and throw it away. It is better for you to enter life maimed or crippled than to have two hands or two feet and be thrown into eternal fire. And if your eye causes you to sin, gouge it out and throw it away. It is better for you to enter life with one eye than to have two eyes and be thrown into the fire of hell." (Matt. 18:8–9)

Can this be the God of love speaking? Most certainly, for that God of love is the Holy God who detests sin. For our own good He wants us to be rid of it, for the unrighteous cannot be one with the Righteous. Anything that stands in the way of God's perfection in our lives is sin.

The way in which He deals with each individual will always be totally just and "the holy God will show himself holy by his righteousness." (Is. 5:16) He does not expect anything of His people that He does not do Himself. He desires to see justice on the earth because He is Himself just. He requires righteous living and actions of His children because He is Himself righteous. He is prepared to lead them to holiness because He is Himself holy.

The difficulty is that some have given their lives to Him,

have accepted Jesus personally as Saviour and expressed their willingness for Him to be the Lord of their lives; they have experienced the working of the Holy Spirit within them and know that they love God; and yet, if they are honest, they have to admit they do not truly want holiness. They are not passionately concerned with the righteousness of God and recognise that many of their thoughts, desires and actions are definitely unrighteous. And when it comes to justice, they have their own concepts of the way in which they believe God should act in their lives; they want to transfer their ideas of justice on to Him instead of seeking to understand His justice.

The Lord will not be exalted by our ideas, only by His own justice. He will always demonstrate His holiness by acting righteously as He deals with nations, the Church, individuals. He cannot deny Himself or act in any way inconsistent with His own nature. To act unjustly, unrighteously or in unholiness would make Him sinful like man and all creation would immediately collapse, for He sustains His creation by His Word, by being faithful and true to what He is. He will not descend to the levels of sin and disobedience. He sent His Son who remained sinless in the midst of sin and disobedience, in order that He might raise us from our sinful state into His divine perfection. He meets with us where we are in order to lead us to His heavenly throne; He accepts us as we are in order to transform us into what He wants us to be.

However, He does expect and look for our cooperation with Him in His divine purposes. We are to love Him for Himself, not only for the benefits we can receive from Him. We will be prepared to settle for His purposes instead of trying to convince Him that ours are better!

God is concerned primarily with what we are rather than what we do. If we are what He wants us to be then we will do what He wants us to do. To try to reform the doing without reforming the heart is, therefore, futile. God starts with the heart.

How much church activity, which is costly in terms of

time and effort, comes to nothing because God will not anoint and prosper what is done in unholiness? How many church fellowships organise their programmes and seek God's blessings upon them, without facing the real issues of what God wants to do in the lives of those who worship Him? How many congregations strive to improve their methods of evangelism without allowing the Lord to do what needs to be done in their own lives so that they will really be leaven in the lump, salt for the earth, light for the world or a city set on a hill that cannot be hidden?

It is easy to fall into the trap of seeking blessing, anointing, provision, healing, forgiveness or anything else that we need to receive from the Lord, without seeking Him for Himself, seeking to draw near to Him, inviting Him to deal with us, to do what he wants, to refine us and make us more like Himself.

It should be self-evident that the more like Jesus we become, the more fruitful we will be in our living, serving, witnessing and evangelising. There is no activity that will not immediately be improved because we have become more like Him.

This does not mean that we wait until we attain some more perfect state before He will use us. From the time of his new birth the Lord will work through a Christian. Despite his imperfections, God will still be able to use the young believer as well as the one who is maturing in the faith, so long as he has a desire to be used.

How much more effectively and fruitfully can He use the one who seeks Him, who cries from his heart: "Lord, I want to be more like you. I want you to deal with the things in my life that are not like you. I want to be holy because you are holy."

He has saved us and called us to a holy life – not because of anything we have done but because of his own purpose and grace.

HOLY PEOPLE

The Lord wants to see corporate holiness in congregations and fellowships. That can only happen if the individuals within those churches are seeking godliness in their personal lives and want their relationships to be holy and loving in the Lord. His warning through Jeremiah is still relevant today: "My people have committed two sins: They have forsaken me, the spring of living water, and have dug their own cisterns, broken cisterns that cannot hold water." (Jer. 2:13)

There is little point in congregations claiming to have life, or trading upon past seasons of blessing. If they have life, it will be obvious to all; the springs of living water will be flowing freely. Outsiders will know they are among a holy people, whose lives are given to the Lord, and among whom He moves in sovereign power.

It is possible to dig our own cisterns and wonder why they cannot contain blessing. Even the blessings that do come seem to pass so rapidly that soon they are only a memory. "'Consider then and realise how evil and bitter it is for you when you forsake the Lord your God and have no awe of me,' declares the Lord, the Lord Almighty." (Jer. 2:19)

Can we say we need no renewal, no revival of our personal and corporate life? Is the world awestruck by the faithfulness, the life and vitality, the holiness and righteousness of Christian churches? How can the world be in awe of Christians, unless they are in awe of their God?

That awe is not a sentimental silence during times of worship. When people are in awe of God they are broken before the Cross, lost in the wonder of adoration and unwilling to walk in the ways that are unholy or unrighteous. There is a keen sense of being the people of God, a true devotion to Him and a loving obedience to His words.

THE CORINTHIAN PROBLEM

In his first letter to Corinth Paul describes the Christians there as "sanctified in Christ Jesus and called to be holy".

(1:2) They have been enriched in every way (1:5), they do not lack any spiritual gift (1:7) and Paul promises that Jesus will keep them strong to the end. (1:8)

And yet what follows in the rest of the letter seems to be a catalogue of unholy disasters. There is division and quarrelling among the believers, sexual immorality is tolerated, some are drunk when they come together for fellowship, and there is confusion in their worship – to name only some of their problems.

These are the people "sanctified in Christ Jesus and called to be holy"! Why should they have spiritual gifts and yet be guilty of many things that are a denial of the life of the Holy Spirit who inspires those gifts? This is a relevant question for today. The renewing activity of the Spirit in churches in recent years has resulted in many Christians coming to a personal experience of joy in worship, use of the Holy Spirit's gifts, a deeper sense of God's love and dimensions of power. And yet, all too often, their new found zeal and enthusiasm for the Lord has not led to a marked evidence of holiness in their lives.

As well as loving the things of the Spirit, some want to hold on to the things of the world. Others can talk avidly of the Christian life without having consecration to live that life. Some want the works of power, the miracles and healings, without the true stamp of God's holiness on their lives.

These things are not true everywhere, but they are common enough for some onlookers to question how much of God is really present in what is known as the renewal of the Holy Spirit. There can be no renewing or reviving of God's people unless it is the work of God Himself. The inadequacies of the Church's witness are obvious to all, whether we speak of those involved in renewal or of the Church generally.

In many ways the Corinthian experience is being repeated, together with problems the Galatians faced. "After beginning with the Spirit, are you now trying to attain your goal by human effort?" (Gal. 3:3) Looking at the Church situation generally, the letters to the churches of Asia Minor recorded in Revelation, chapters 2 and 3, are as relevant today as when they were written. It is Ephesus, Sardis and Laodicea all over again. The problems the Church faces today are not new in essence, only in form. And the scriptures therefore speak directly to the Church in its needs today.

EPHESUS

To the church at Ephesus, the Holy Spirit said: "Yet I hold this against you: You have forsaken your first love. Remember the height from which you have fallen! Repent and do the things you did at first. If you do not repent, I will come to you and remove your lampstand from its place." (Rev. 2:4–5)

Both Ephesus and Sardis are warned that things will become worse, not better, unless there is repentance. They need to respond to the Word of God. Revival does not happen by people expecting the Lord to meet suddenly with the congregation, while they sit back waiting for something to happen. Those people need to be on their faces before the Lord crying to Him to revive them. The Lord cannot be glorified in a complacent church.

Knowing evangelical truths does not bring revival either; only a seeking of God for Himself can produce a suitable climate for God to move in sovereign power. A congregation can be well taught and yet not be performing the deeds the Lord is looking for. The Word needs to be received, heard and obeyed.

LAODICEA

To Laodicea the Spirit writes words often quoted today: "I know your deeds, that you are neither cold nor hot. I wish you were either one or the other! So, because you are lukewarm – neither hot nor cold – I am about to spit you out of my mouth. You say, 'I am rich; I have acquired

wealth and do not need a thing.' But you do not realise that
you are wretched, pitiful, poor, blind and naked. I counsel
you to buy from me gold refined in the fire, so you can
become rich; and white clothes to wear, so that you can
cover your shameful nakedness; and salve to put on your
eyes, so that you can see. Those whom I love I rebuke and
discipline. So be earnest, and repent." (Rev. 3:15–19)

The Lord sees things very differently from the Christians
at Laodicea. They are content and have all they desire. God
sees unholiness, the need for refining, cleansing and anointing. It is in His love for those who profess a love for Him
that He rebukes and disciplines them calling them to
repentance.

REVIVAL NEEDED

The message for today is clear. If the nation is to be revived
spiritually, morally, socially and even politically and econo-
mically, there must be revival in the Church. That begins
with corporate repentance, confessing the sin of not revealing Jesus to this generation and giving ourselves
wholeheartedly to Him that our hearts may be made pure,
our pride and selfishness broken and our lives anointed. We
cannot expect revival in the nation until there is revival in
the Church. And there will not be revival in the Church
without genuine repentance and desire for personal holiness.

God has sanctified us in Christ Jesus and has called us to
be holy. His work of sanctification is continuing in our lives.
The reason why we do not manifest the holy life of Jesus
more fully is due, first, to a lack of repentance – of grieving
over our sin and earnestly desiring the transforming work
of holiness in our lives.

Second, there is little brokenness. We want the blessings
of the Lord, but we also want to fulfil our own desires for
our lives. Our wills are not sufficiently submitted to His.

Third, there are few who see the anointing of the holiness
of Jesus in their lives: the work of the Holy Spirit that will

cause them to manifest more of Him in their characters and daily action.

In recent years people have been seeking the Lord for experiences of the Holy Spirit: His power, love, gifts, healings, joy, etc. But how many have truly been seeking Him for the holiness that God wants the spirit to bring into their lives?

No words could be more appropriate than those Paul wrote in his second letter to Corinth: "Let us purify ourselves from everything that contaminates body and spirit, perfecting holiness out of reverence for God." (7:1) Then we can expect to see the Gospel having more impact on modern society. For a holy people will be salt for the earth, light for the world, leaven in the lump and a city set on a hill that cannot be hidden.

Let us purify ourselves from everything that contaminates body and spirit, perfecting holiness out of reverence for God.

LEADERS

People will follow where they are led. Leaders in the Church have great responsibility: "Remember your leaders, who spoke the word of God to you. Consider the outcome of their way of life and imitate their faith." (Heb. 13:7)

Leaders have three responsibilities. First, they are to "speak the word of God". This they cannot do effectively unless they are themselves men of the Word. To speak the Word of God is not to tickle people's ears with an amusing sermonette on a Sunday morning. It is to bring God's Word prophetically to people, both from Scripture and by the Holy Spirit; the particular word that God is speaking to His people in that place at that time. This implies the leader has sensitivity to the voice of the Spirit and willingness to proclaim what He says, regardless of the desires or reactions of the people.

There needs to be a prophetic element in preaching, but prophecy and preaching should not be confused. Not all preaching is prophetic and the leader will need to be prophetic when he is not preaching, for he has the responsibility of speaking God's Word into the lives of those he leads, individually as well as corporately.

Second, a leader demonstrates the words that he proclaims. Consider the outcome of his way of life. The people will not follow unless they are led BY EXAMPLE. They will not heed the man who says one thing but does another. You would not believe the salesman who had great claims for his product, if the product did not measure up to his words.

People look for example in their pastors, and rightly so. He needs to be proficient in many things they find difficult so that he may teach them. He needs to be a man of prayer as well as the Word, a man of faith and love and obedience; a man in whom they can see something of Jesus.

Leaders who allow themselves to be manipulated by others will lead their people nowhere. To give an example of holiness they will need to keep their eyes on the Lord and be concerned to please Him. Jesus was uncompromising in doing the will of His Father who sent Him – and He led the holy life.

Third, leaders are to be men of faith. They not only proclaim the Word of God, they believe it and will not compromise its implications to please men. They show what it is to trust the Lord in trying and testing circumstances. Their faith is not in the problems but in the One who is the answer to those problems.

The true leader is not afraid to step out in obedience to the Word brought by the Spirit. He believes "Jesus Christ is the same yesterday and today and forever." (Heb. 13:8) He learns that God will challenge him before dealing with the people. He must be the first to respond to what He is saying; then he can encourage others in their faith, drawing their eyes towards Jesus and away from self-concern, self-consciousness, self-pity and all the other aspects of self-life which are a denial of their holy calling.

The people, for their part, are to obey their leaders, "so that their work will be a joy, not a burden." (Heb. 13:17) They will be ready to do that when they see the Lord's authority in their lives; they will be men of authority only if they are submitted to the Lord's authority. Ecclesiastical appointment will not give them that authority, only submission to His will.

PAUL'S ADVICE TO LEADERS

Timothy was a young Christian leader. In his letters to him Paul makes it clear that godliness must be the foundation of his life and ministry. He describes Timothy as "my true son in the faith" and tells him that God's work can only be accomplished in love, "which comes from a pure heart and a good conscience and a sincere faith". (1 Tim. 1:5)

Paul urges Timothy to "fight the good fight, holding on to faith and a good conscience," and warns that "some have rejected these and so have shipwrecked their faith." (1 Tim. 1:18–19) Conscience warns us when we are likely to grieve God. To drown the voice of conscience is dangerous for we almost certainly will fall into disobedience if we do. The conscience of a Christian is informed by God's Word and every believer has the responsibility, therefore, to be well informed about that Word.

"Train yourself to be godly," Paul says. The Christian life is like that of an athlete who needs to be in strict training in order to win the prize. "Pursue righteousness, godliness, faith, love, endurance and gentleness," Paul says. Run after them, chase them, determined to achieve them. He is not to allow anything to deter him from his personal quest for these characteristics – then he will be able to influence others, giving them an example of holiness: "Set an example for the believers in speech, in life, in love, in faith and in purity." (1 Tim. 4:12)

Are we to assume that Timothy was particularly prone to ungodliness? Not at all! Paul was well aware of the pressures on leaders and he wanted to safeguard his spiritual son from dangers which would undermine his ministry. More than that, he wished to impress upon him that his effectiveness in ministry would depend upon his walk of holiness.

The grace of God "teaches us to say 'No' to ungodliness and worldly passions, and to live self-controlled, upright and godly lives in this present age." (Tit. 2:12) In his letters to Timothy and Titus, Paul puts considerable emphasis on self-control which is part of the fruit of the Holy Spirit. The self-life that opposes the Spirit must be kept under control so they are free to do the positive good that God asks of them.

The weighty responsibilities that rest upon leaders in the Church should not cause them to despair, but to trust increasingly in the ministry and power of the Holy Spirit. It cannot be emphasised enough that any attempt to train yourself to be godly, keep yourself pure, pursue righteousness, godliness, faith, love, endurance and gentleness, or even to exercise self-control, that is attempted in your own strength will inevitably fail.

Holiness is allowing the Spirit of God's holiness placed within us to shine through our lives. All leaders are to demonstrate lives full of Jesus; it is to be seen clearly by all that they are men of the Spirit.

How sad that one often hears such questions as: "Is he a Christian?" "Is he born again?" "Is he open to the power of the Spirit?" Such questions are unnecessary of those who radiate the life of God's Spirit. "He is a man of the Spirit," it is said.

No wonder Christians are urged to pray for their leaders, for they are responsible to God for the way they lead His people. They will have to stand before His throne and give account for their own walk of holiness, faith and love, and the example they have given to others.

Pursue righteousness, faith, love, and peace, along with all those who call on the Lord out of a pure heart.

20. THE FIGHT OF FAITH

Some Christians today, who want an instant form of Christianity full of power and drama but lacking in depth, will not want to face up to what God is saying about holiness. On the other hand there are many who have tasted power, miracles, healings, love and joy, new heights of praise – and yet yearn for more. They recognise how little of Jesus is seen in some aspects of their lives; they long for a closer walk with the one they love.

It is not a question of holding the miraculous power of God over against His holiness. The Holy God is Almighty, and the Almighty God is Holy. He wants His children to know His gifts, power, miracles, healings, love, joy, praise – AND holiness – in their lives.

The mature Christian learns to add new dimensions of God's wholeness to his experience without losing what he already knows of Him. He lives a life of continual consecration and faith: "Then Joshua told the people, 'Consecrate yourselves, for tomorrow the Lord will do åmazing things among you.'" (Josh. 3:5)

Holiness and Almightiness go together in God and both are linked in the lives of Christians. If we worship a holy, awesome God, then we should expect to see Him doing holy, awesome things among His people. As we consecrate ourselves to Him we can expect Him to do the amazing things He loves to do among those who trust Him. The saints of God will "tell of the glory of your kingdom and speak of your might, so that all men may know of your

mighty acts and the glorious splendour of your kingdom."
(Ps. 145:11–12)

How can Christians tell of the glory of God's Kingdom
unless they taste of that glory now? How can they speak of
God's might unless they taste for themselves something of
His powerful ways? And in Scripture this is seen as the
responsibility of every generation of believers.

Some seem to think that they will only know that glory
and power beyond their physical death. It will be too late
then to speak of these things to others! The opportunity of
witness in this world will be gone.

They will speak of the glorious splendour of your majesty,
    and I will meditate on your wonderful works.
They will tell of the power of your awesome works,
    and I will proclaim your great deeds.
They will celebrate your abundant goodness
    and joyfully sing of your righteousness.

(Ps. 145:5–7)

The saints of every generation, including this one, can only
"speak of the glorious splendour of your majesty" if they
know that majesty for themselves. They can only "tell of
the power of your awesome works" because they see those
works being performed in their own experience.

David can testify: "I will meditate on your wonderful
works," "I will proclaim your great deeds." This is the
responsibility of all saints and he was able to fulfil his part in
it.

The closer we draw to the Lord in His holiness, the
greater our awareness of His almightiness. We see the
circumstances of our lives from His position instead of our
own and mountains become pimples. Our faith is enlarged
to believe our mighty God will deal not only with the
unholy things we see in our own lives, but also with the

situations where nothing less than a miracle will suffice.

It is sad that in the history of the Church there should have been so many divisions caused by believers emphasising certain aspects of the truth to the neglect of others, even denying aspects of the truth that are beyond their personal experience. This is the continuing sin of denominationalism.

ONE SPIRIT

The mature believer has learned to recognise "there are different kinds of gifts, but the same Spirit. There are different kinds of service, but the same Lord. There are different kinds of working, but the same God works all of them in all men." (1 Cor. 12:4–6) He is keen to recognise the way in which He is working in other believers and fellowships, even though there may be differences in doctrine and attitudes towards many aspects of the Christian life.

None of us understands or manifests the whole truth. The Holy Spirit is given to guide us into all truth. He wants us to bring together in our personal and corporate lives the different aspects of His truth.

He wants to see the love of Jesus in you. He wants to see the anointing of joy on your life and His peace in your heart. He wants to see His love in operation as you humbly serve others. He desires to see you expressing faith in His Word by the things you say and do, as well as in the way you pray. He wants to see His mighty power at work; His supernatural power released in the daily circumstances of your life. He longs for you to have relationships that please Him, a marriage that honours Him, a home where His authority presides. He rejoices when your fellowship expresses corporately the life, love, power and forgiveness of Jesus.

THE DIMENSION OF FAITH

In other words, He loves to see holiness, because He is holy. He is not concerned to see certain aspects of His holy life, but His fullness expressed in your life. Praise Him for all that He has already done for you. What is lacking? Is there faith to believe God to heal, to perform miracles and do mighty things in your life? That relates as much to holiness as living in moral correctness, because God has called you to a life of faith. Without faith it is impossible to please God and it is the man who continues to live by faith who receives the Lord's salvation.

When you live by faith you believe God to intervene in power in the circumstances of your life. Then you have a constant testimony of His mighty acts and are able to tell of what He is doing by His Kingly power.

If you see the Lord blessing others in ways lacking in your own life, begin to seek Him to provide for you in that way. The fullness of His life is yours in Jesus. He does not want you to concentrate only on those aspects of His life that are already familiar to you. As you grow in maturity He wants to add those dimensions lacking in your experience.

Ask Him to show you your blind spots, your needs that you refuse to recognise; or any wrong attitudes to other believers. Are you trying to justify the fact that you do not manifest aspects of Jesus' life clearly seen in them? Or are you prepared to seek the Lord so that He will add those dimensions to your experience of Him? Give yourself afresh to Him that He may give Himself afresh to you.

Consecrate yourselves, for tomorrow the Lord will do amazing things among you.

FIGHT

Paul's advice to Timothy and Titus holds good for all Christians, not only for leaders. He tells Timothy to "Fight the good fight of the faith." (1 Tim. 6:12) You will need to be a fighter in your Christian life if you are going to overcome temptation, conquer doubt, be obedient and love in every situation.

The flesh will always be opposed to the Spirit and will demand your attention. You will need to resist its desires to be the controlling interest in your life, reckoning yourself dead to the old life. Remember, Jesus did not try to reform your flesh but came so you could be a new creation led by the Spirit.

Satan will not miss any opportunities that you give him and he will use any temptation he can to lure you from the purposes of God. The fight is not only the internal struggle against sin, pride and selfishness. "Our struggle is not against flesh and blood, but against the rulers, against the authorities, against the powers of this dark world and against the spiritual forces of evil in the heavenly realms." (Eph. 6:12)

You will need to engage in spiritual warfare against those "spiritual forces of evil in the heavenly realms" so that you do not come under any false condemnation or accusation, or allow the enemy to oppress you with spiritual heaviness.

The world will continue to try and impress its values upon you. It is a fight to resist conforming to this present world and to ensure that our values are those of Jesus. It is much easier to place yourself in the ways of temptation than resist it, or to go along with others for fear of appearing different.

Satan is God's enemy and yours too. He will do all he can to stir your flesh and place before you worldly things that would entice you. So every Christian is called to be a soldier, whether he likes the idea or not.

The best method of defence is attack. If we passively allow the enemy to hurl everything at us without fighting then we will soon feel crushed and defeated. If, however, we use the sword of the Spirit, which is the Word of God, and move on to the offensive we can have the victory over Satan. We have been given spiritual weapons to pull down his strongholds.

The Christian life is not one of comfortable ease. That is the passive state that Satan loves to see in the lives of those who claim to follow Christ. If they do not fight against the temptations of the flesh, they will give in to them: greed, lust, anger, jealousy etc . . .

If the believer is afraid of the world, he will be a poor witness. He will fear ridicule and criticism; he will often choose the easy way of appearing to be one with the world, instead of demonstrating that he is a child of the Kingdom who opposes the corrupt standards around him. If he does not fight worldliness, he becomes part of it.

CLEAR CONSCIENCE

Paul encourages his young brother in the Lord, Timothy, to be vigilant in this good fight. He will need to hold fast to the Lord Jesus, knowing His presence is continually with him, His power available to him. However, no Christian can have adequate trust in His presence if his own conscience condemns him. So Paul's advice is to walk with the Lord with a clear conscience and he will then be able to have complete trust and confidence in Him, no matter what situation he finds himself in.

Those who do not fight and have allowed their consciences to be strained, "have shipwrecked their faith". They obviously are not living at the Cross with the fresh cleansing of the precious blood of Jesus that washes consciences clean from all guilt. Stubborn refusal to repent is tantamount to a determination to fight against the will of God, instead of fighting the good fight against sin, the world and the devil.

It is only by engaging in the fight that we can know true peace. Paul tells Timothy to pray for others "that we may live peaceful and quiet lives in all godliness and holiness." (1 Tim. 2:2)

THE FIGHT OF FAITH

The fight is essentially one of faith: to believe God, His Word and promises, over and above the trying circumstances and setbacks that all Christians inevitably encounter; to know that He will carry you through all the trials of your faith: "Consider it pure joy, my brothers, whenever you face trials of many kinds, because you know that the testing of your faith develops perseverance. Perseverance must finish its work so that you may be mature and complete, not lacking anything." (James 1:2–4)

Without perseverance there can be no ultimate victory, only a series of sad defeats. Without the good fight of faith there will be no perseverance.

Paul himself fought with purpose: "I do not fight like a man beating the air." (1 Cor. 9:26) Instead he likens the Christian to a runner who must be in strict training to gain the prize, "a crown that will last forever". (v. 25)

The fight of faith is a disciplined fight, not relaxing vigilance so that the enemy can record even a minor victory. "Thanks be to God, who always leads us in triumphal procession in Christ." (2 Cor. 2:14) In Jesus there can be no defeat; so when we abide in Him we do not experience defeat no matter what trying circumstances we have to encounter.

However, that does not mean we are to feel condemned at every failure. That would give the enemy a double victory. As soon as we realise we have stumbled we can turn immediately to Jesus and claim the cleansing of His blood, so there can be no condemnation for us. That failure can encourage us to be even more determined in our fight of faith.

God does not want us to become discouraged. When we see needs in our lives, it is easy to pray that God will immediately resolve the whole situation with one sweep of His almighty hand. Sometimes we have faith to believe Him to do that; often we do not.

When that is the case it is helpful to set yourself a faith-goal. What improvement in the situation do you believe that there will be within a week? Be clear about your answer and don't set your sights too high. Pray for God's grace to see that faith-goal realised.

When that is attained you will discover that God has

given you faith for the next step and then the next, and so on. If you want to move from one side of a large room to the other, you do not try to leap the distance in one giant jump. You take one step after another until you reach your destination.

You might want God to convert the entire nation, which would be a noble intention; but you do not have the faith that He will. However, He can give you faith for your neighbour to come to know Him, or for a dozen or more to be added to your fellowship.

Remember that Jesus is the Author and Perfector or Finisher of your faith. Respond to His initiative and if He gives you vision for a particular purpose, do not give up the fight of faith until you see that goal realised.

Paul could say: "I have fought the good fight, I have finished the race, I have kept the faith. Now there is in store for me the crown of righteousness, which the Lord, the righteous Judge, will award to me on that day – and not only to me, but also to all who have longed for his appearing." (2 Tim. 4:7–8)

Are there situations to which you have reacted passively? Are you allowing the enemy to push you around, to make you feel condemned and useless? If so, it is time to fight. He who is in you, the Holy Spirit, is greater than he who is in the world, Satan. You have authority over the powers of darkness because you belong to the Kingdom of God and they do not. When you fight, there is no fear of losing. You are proclaiming the victory of Jesus over a defeated foe.

Fight the good fight of faith.

21. WORSHIP

It is in worship, adoration and praise that we come into the Holy presence of the Lord, joining with heavenly hosts that declare His praises eternally:

> Holy, holy holy,
> is the Lord God Almighty,
> who was, and is, and is to come.
> (Rev. 4:8)

Those closest to the throne declare the Holiness and Almightiness of God day and night: "You are worthy, our Lord and God, to receive glory and honour and power." (Rev. 4:11) Jesus, raised to glory and majesty is worshipped as the Lamb who gave His life for us that we might have entrance into those hallowed courts of praise: "Worthy is the Lamb, who was slain, to receive power and wealth and wisdom and strength and honour and glory and praise." (Rev. 5:12)

What a joy and privilege to be able to come into those courts of praise now and know the living God, to fall down before Him in adoration and praise, looking forward to that time when we will be able to enjoy Him without the temptations of the world, the flesh and the devil. "To him who sits on the throne and to the Lamb be praise and honour and glory and power, for ever and ever. The four living creatures said, 'Amen' and the elders fell down and worshipped." (Rev. 5:13–14)

Those are words sung by "every creature in heaven and on earth and under the earth and on the sea, and all that is in them". When God reveals Himself, all creation has to

declare His praise. Men could not remain silent, neither
could they remain on their feet. If the heavenly beings fall
on their faces before the holiness of God, we who dwell in
the midst of unholiness, will certainly find that necessary:
"All the angels were standing around the throne and
around the elders and the four living creatures. They fell
down on their faces before the throne and worshipped
God, saying: 'Amen! Praise and glory and wisdom and
thanks and honour and power and strength be to our God
for ever and ever. Amen!'" (Rev. 7:11–12)

That company of the heavenly host consists of those who
are cleansed and purified by the blood of the Lamb, made
holy through His atoning sacrifice. "These are they who
have come out of the great tribulation; they have washed
their robes and made them white in the blood of the Lamb.
Therefore, they are before the throne of God and serve
him day and night in his temple; and he who sits on the
throne will spread his tent over them. Never again will they
hunger; never again will they thirst. The sun will not beat
upon them, nor any scorching heat. For the Lamb at the
centre of the throne will be their shepherd; he will lead
them to springs of living water. And God will wipe away
every tear from their eyes." (Rev. 7:14–17)

These are promises for the faithful children of God. The
wonder is that we can begin to meet with the Lord in His
holiness NOW when we hunger to do so, when we long to
come into His holy presence and are willing to humble
ourselves before Him like the heavenly host. What we
know of Him now is nothing compared to what we shall
know then: "Then I shall know fully, even as I am fully
known." (1 Cor. 13:12)

> O worship the Lord in the beauty of holiness!
>   Bow down before him, his glory proclaim.
> With gold of obedience, and incense of lowliness,
>   Kneel and adore him, the Lord is his name!
>   (J. S. B. Mansell)

Holy, holy, holy, is the Lord God almighty, who was, and is, and is to come.

EXPERIENCE OF WORSHIP

Even though our present awareness of God's holiness is so imperfect, we can rejoice that He is always present among His people. "Shout aloud and sing for joy, people of Zion, for great is the Holy One of Israel among you." (Is. 12:6)

The worship many Christians experience as the norm is far different from that of the New Testament. Congregations stand and sing politely: "Holy, holy, holy, Lord God Almighty." How often do people fall on their faces as they sing because they are so aware of the holiness of the God to whom they address the words? That would probably be regarded as undignified, improper even. The minister might point out that everything is to be done "decently and in order". Is that to suggest that the heavenly host do not worship decently and in order? In heaven all fall on their faces before the living God and that is the experience of God's people here on earth when they draw near to His holy presence.

Should we not long for the day when we see congregations on their faces before God as He touches lives with His cleansing and sanctifying power?

The Scriptures suggest that there is also an exaltant praise when God's people are so aware of His glory, His victory and power, that they can no longer refrain from shouting His praises. Is this to be regarded as disorderly? Is this emotionalism or over-exuberance? It is certainly very different from falling before the throne of God in adoration but it is equally scriptural.

How anaemic so much of our hymn and chorus singing seems to be in comparison with New Testament worship. Men's love of order makes it difficult for the Spirit of God to move spontaneously among His people, to lead the worship and inspire the worshippers. It is one thing to pray for such inspiration at the beginning of the service; it is quite another to let it happen.

There will be those who try to initiate what the Spirit gives spontaneously, but imitations never work. How ungodly it would be for a congregation to start shouting praises as a contrivance to fulfil the Scriptures instead of letting the Spirit lead the people to that place of exaltant praise where it seems they are joining with the eternal shouts of heaven.

Would it be real for a minister to suggest that the people prostrate themselves before the Lord if the Spirit has not led them to that place of humbling themselves before God in awe of His holiness?

It can be real for people to cry out for God's mercy when under conviction of the Holy Spirit. How empty for people to ask for mercy when there is no desire for it. May the Lord save us from imitations of true worship. How many hearts are left empty and needs unmet because those attending services have had no true encounter with God? Should not the people of God come together every Sunday to seek the holy face of the Lord God, rather than do their religious duty by attending a service?

What may not be possible in the congregation on Sunday (because not all are willing to seek the Lord) is certainly possible at other times if small groups of Christians are prepared to gather, not for conventional prayer meetings, but literally to seek the face of God. Conventional prayer meetings rarely accomplish that, for to seek the face of the Lord means that He will deal first with the worshippers before drawing them into the place of intercession before His throne.

We come into that place through the Cross, experiencing afresh the reviving power of God, conviction of sin, repentance, forgiveness, a new awareness of His grace, love and mercy. We humble ourselves before Him in repentant awe. It is then that God calls upon His people to pray for His Church and the world, for the lost and all who do not have access to that holy place through the blood of Jesus.

The Lord who draws us into His presence to worship Him, always gives back an abundance of Himself to us: "For this is what the high and lofty One says – he who lives forever, whose name is holy: 'I live in a high and holy place, but also with him who is contrite and lowly in spirit, to revive the spirit of the lowly and to revive the heart of the contrite.' " (Is. 57:15)

Holy, holy, holy, is the Lord God almighty, who was, and is, and is to come.

SANCTIFIED BY TRUTH

We are "set apart" for God. We do not belong to the world, we do not even belong to ourselves. We belong to our heavenly Father. Like Jesus, our citizenship is in heaven. We are part of His Kingdom.

When Jesus prayed for His disciples before His arrest, He said: "They are not of the world, even as I am not of it. Sanctify them by the truth; your word is truth. As you sent me into the world, I have sent them into the world. For them I sanctify myself, that they too may be truly sanctified." (John 17:16–19)

Disciples need to be consecrated to Him, fully given and yielded to Him, desiring to live God's Kingdom life, recognising His authority in their lives. They need to maintain their consecration, persevering through all opposition that lies ahead of them, by giving themselves to Him, and humbly bending to His will, saying "Yes" to whatever He asks of them.

If you stop giving yourself to the Lord, you will inevitably fall back into self-pleasing. That is to live in the flesh rather than the Spirit.

Jesus was continually impressing on the disciples that what He is, they were to be, what He did, they were to do. We can understand their reluctance to believe such possibilities. Nevertheless He was preparing them to be His Body in the world when He had returned to His Father's glory.

Because He is holy, we are to be holy;
Because He is righteous, we are to walk in righteousness;
Because He is just, we are to be just in all our ways,
Because He is mighty, we are to see His mighty acts in our
　　experience.
Because He is gracious, we are to be gracious;
Because He is merciful to us, we are to be merciful to
　　others.
Because He is love, we are to love Him and others
　　wholeheartedly.
Because He is faithful, we are called to be faithful.

Revival begins, not in the world, but in God's own
people. Their hearts are revived, brought back to life with
the holiness and love of Jesus. A necessary condition for
such revival is repentance for all that is unholy in the
believer's life. Some of these things he may be aware of;
others will be hidden from him because the heart is so
deceitful. There will be deep motives of pride and selfishness which he may not recognise, but which lie behind all
he does in the name of God.

The saints are those who celebrate the abundant goodness of the Lord. Holiness is not a burden of restrictions to
be borne by the believer – but liberation from all burdens,
freedom to celebrate God's abundant goodness and to
joyfully sing of His righteousness. The Lord has been
gracious and compassionate to them because He is "slow to
anger and rich in love". (Ps. 145:8)

"Will you not revive us again, that your people may
rejoice in you? Show us your unfailing love, O Lord, and
grant us your salvation." (Ps. 85:5–6)

In Him: "Love and faithfulness meet together; righteousness and peace kiss each other." (Ps. 85:10) That is a
beautiful description of the personal revival that comes
with a Christian's life when he seeks God in His holy power.
"Exalt the Lord our God and worship at His footstool; he
is holy . . . Exalt the Lord our God and worship at his holy
mountain, for the Lord our God is holy." (Ps. 99:5,9)

God calls His children to a life of service as well as worship. As Jesus was sent into the world by His Father, so He sends us to be His witnesses in the world. We are not to be conformed to this present world or we will not be leaven in the lump, the salt of the earth or light for the world. Jesus was well aware of the great difficulties that would be facing the disciples. They would need unity and holiness if their witness in the world was to be effective.

I SANCTIFY MYSELF

Jesus prays: "For them I sanctify myself, that they too may be truly sanctified." (John 17:19) When Jesus speaks of sanctifying Himself He uses the word in the sense of consecrating Himself entirely to His Father's will and purpose. He needed to do that as He was faced with the necessity of crucifixion. He endured the agony in the Garden of Gethsemane, when in His humanity He wanted to avoid the cup of suffering, but in obedience prayed: "Yet not my will, but yours be done." (Luke 22:42) That is the prayer of consecration.

This is not a phrase to be added to the end of every prayer as a safety valve in case we do not receive what we ask for. Used like that these words only betray a lack of faith on the part of the one praying. No, these are the words of con-secration. We will need to pray them whenever we are confronted by God with something that we would much rather avoid. For the saint will prefer the will of His Father to his own, even if that involves considerable personal cost.

Those Christians involved in costly ministry are willing to face the cost because of their love for God. Pleasing Him is what matters. The cost involved is outweighed by knowing they are being obedient. Even when they are weary be-cause of the cost, they do not give up. For the way of love is the way of obedience.

Jesus could not say "I sanctify myself" in the sense of making Himself pure by cleansing Himself of impurity. He had no sin, no impurity, there was nothing imperfect about

Him. He was willing to sanctify Himself completely, to consecrate Himself, to offer His life wholeheartedly to the Father even to the point of dying on the Cross – that His disciples "may be truly sanctified". For it is only by the shedding of His blood that we can be cleansed from every sin and brought into the holiness of God.

We are pure in His sight, sanctified by Jesus. Nothing encourages you to live in holiness more than the realisation that God regards you as holy. This is His calling upon your life. When you know this in your heart, you are willing to consecrate yourself to Him again and again that you may live as one yielded to Him and who, by His grace, will remain faithful to Him.

There is much at stake, for your obedience can have a powerful impact on many other people. If there is to be a spiritual awakening in the nation, there will need to be personal revival among God's children. The revival that many pray for has to begin in their own hearts and lives.

REVIVAL IN THE NATIONS

The Lord works out His purpose in the nations, in His Church and in each of our lives, for His own sake: "This is what the Sovereign Lord says: It is not for your sake, O house of Israel, that I am going to do those things, but for the sake of my holy name. . . . I will show the holiness of my great name, which has been profaned among the nations, the name you have profaned among them. Then the nations will know that I am the Lord, declares the Sovereign Lord, when I show myself holy through you before their eyes." (Ezek. 36:22–23)

God draws us to Himself in holiness for His own sake, to see His children reflecting His holiness. He enables us to be faithful, to reflect His holiness in the world. The nations shall know that God has been at work among His people: "Then the nations . . . will know that I the Lord have rebuilt what was destroyed and have replanted what was desolate. I the Lord have spoken and I will do it." (v. 36)

We are left with a greater sense of wonder that this holy God should want anything to do with unholy men. Thankfully, God has supplied a Saviour so that we will not die, but live eternally in His holy presence. We can identify with the great song of praise that came from the lips of Mary:

> My soul praises the Lord
>   and my spirit rejoices in God my Saviour,
> for he has been mindful of the humble state of his
>   servant.
> From now on all generations will call me blessed,
>   for the Mighty One has done great things for
>   me –
>   holy is his name.
> His mercy extends to those who fear him,
>   from generation to generation.
> He has performed mighty deeds with his arm;
>   he has scattered those who are proud in their
>   inmost thoughts.
> He has brought down rulers from their thrones
>   but has lifted up the humble.
> He has filled the hungry with good things
>   but has sent the rich away empty.
>   (Luke 1:46–53)

The name of God in Scripture denotes the person of God. His name is Holy, because He is holy. Jesus prayed: "Holy Father, protect them by the power of your name." (John 17:11) The Lord calls you to live in His holiness; you are protected by the power of His Holy name. He wants to fill you with good things as you hunger after Him. You will continue to experience Him breaking you of pride and selfishness, and you will know His mercy and mighty acts in your life.

See your personal life in the context in which God sees you. You are His child, precious in His sight. You are also part of the Body of Christ, those who are called together to demonstrate the life of Jesus in the world and to show His truth and love with others. He has a particular part for you to play in that.

He sees you living in Christ and His Spirit living in you and He calls you to a life of worship. "Therefore, I urge you, brothers in view of God's mercy, to offer your bodies as living sacrifices, holy and pleasing to God – which is your spiritual worship." (Rom. 12:1) Every day He is to be pre-eminent in your life. If He is, you will rejoice to humble yourself in His holy presence or to stand in the midst of a praising people who ascribe to Him the honour of which He is worthy.

For them I sanctify myself, that they too may be truly sanctified.

REVIVAL FIRES

Many are praying that God will light fires of revival in the land. By now it should be apparent that His reviving purposes need to start in our own hearts and lives as we welcome His refining activity. We do not need to fear the consuming fire if we submit to the refining fire of His love, purging and cleansing the sin out of our lives. That He always deals with us in love is beyond question, even when we find it difficult to understand why He allows the more traumatic experiences we encounter. However, we only have to look at ourselves briefly to wonder why He bothers with us. We wonder at His amazing grace, the extent of His love and the boundless mercy He extends to us daily.

Life sometimes seems hard; Jesus does not promise it will be easy. However, in Him we can experience victory now and the ultimate triumph when we are raised to eternal glory with Him. It is then that the work of each of us will be tested by fire. Because we know the Lord's acceptance and forgiveness, that He sanctifies those He justifies, we do not need to fear the final outcome, so long as we are prepared to cooperate with Him in the purpose He has for our lives.

Certainly, Jesus does not do more refining in our lives

than is necessary. There is no point in resenting our difficulties. We can see God deal with us in every one of them, always ready to release faith in our hearts to believe Him to overcome the problems.

Allowing God to deal with you is a tiny part of His grand design for the nations. To Him you are not insignificant; you matter because He loves you. Anyone who is the object of God's love is of great importance to Him. He wants to see His purpose for you and all His children fulfilled so that the fire of His Spirit's activity may spread throughout the nation. In working His refining purpose in your life, God is working to bless others through you as His priorities are established in your daily walk with Him.

You walk with the God who is holy. You live in the God who is holy. You talk with the God who is holy. You draw nearer and nearer to the God who is holy. The closer you are to Him, the more like Him you will be and the more able to draw others to His love.

I counsel you to buy from me gold refined in the fire, so you can become rich.

Colin Urquhart

FAITH FOR THE FUTURE

After five richly-blessed years at St. Hugh's, Luton, Colin Urquhart felt that God was calling him to a new ministry – to be 'heard among the nations'. His step of faith into the unknown was the start of a miraculous adventure. Colin's international ministry of renewal, healing and evangelism is now touching and transforming lives all over the world. Revival is brought to others because it has been experienced in the community at the Hyde, where those working with Colin have become freshly aware of the holiness and glory of God.

Faith for the Future is the remarkable and inspiring sequel to *When the Spirit Comes*.

Colin Urquhart

IN CHRIST JESUS

'Wherever I travel I come across "defeated" Christians. Should they have to resign themselves to such defeat? Is it possible to know victory over temptation, weakness, futility and spiritual inadequacy?' asks Colin Urquhart.

In Christ Jesus offers, not new forms of healing or new prayer techniques, but a clear, thrilling statement of what God has done for mankind through Jesus. Some have been Christians for many years and although familiar with the Scriptures, have never learned how to live in the power of these truths, or to be set free by them.

Colin Urquhart here gives the heart of his teaching: how we can know Christ's power for ourselves.

Colin Urquhart

ANYTHING YOU ASK

This book is strong meat. It will be talked about, argued about, and can revolutionise your life.

Jesus makes many astonishing promises of the response that God's children can expect to their prayers. But experience, for many Christians, seems to fall far short. Why?

Here is the teaching of Jesus on prayer and faith. Colin Urquhart shows, with examples from his personal ministry, how people can learn to pray with faith and see God answering their prayers.